THE 3+1 PLAN

The Insider's Way to Achieve

Financial Freedom with Just 4 Properties

The 3+1 Plan
Property is the new Pension

The Insider's Way to Achieve
Financial Freedom with Just 4 Properties

BY BRETT ALEGRE-WOOD

dp

DELANCEY PRESS LONDON, 2009

Published by Delancey Press Ltd.
23 Berkeley Square
London W1J 6HE
www.delanceypress.com

A CIP catalogue record for this title is available from the British Library.

First published 2009
2nd edition

Edited by: Peter Carvell
Jacket by: e-Digital Design
Typesetting and design: Boulevard Studio
Printed and bound by: TJ International

ISBN: 978 0 9539 119 8 1

Acknowledgements

This book is dedicated to the many families that have trusted my guidance, listened to my experience, invested wisely and profited from it.

To the mentors, who guided me through the early years while I found my feet in the world.

To my parents, Kevin and Annette, and my brothers, Daniel and Dean, who supported me while I found my passion.

A special thanks to Murray Gray, best mate and business partner, who originally gave me the idea of an educational blog and who has created and managed my online presence since the beginning of the World Wide Web.

To Simon Shankland, another best mate and business partner, who has worked alongside me and applied the principles for himself and for our clients.

To Alana Alegre, my sister–in–law and Marketing Director, who has been responsible for bringing the book together.

To my team, who have supported our clients and helped them to create a plethora of stories.

And finally, to Arlene, my wife. She is the greatest of supporters and allows me the freedom to achieve my dreams.

Table of Contents

WELCOME TO THE WONDERFUL WORLD OF PROPERTY INVESTMENT

In **The 3+1 Plan** I am offering you an answer to the great challenge that we all face at some moment in our lives. If you are like me, this can be summed up in three simple questions:

- *How can I achieve a more secure financial life for the time when I want to work less or to start retirement?*
- *How can I achieve this without it taking up too much of my time?*
- *And how can I achieve this while having a better lifestyle along the way?*

My answer is **The 3+1 Plan.** That is my shorthand for building a portfolio of four properties.

I believe that with 3 properties to rent and 1 to live in as your home, you can achieve your financial future without wasting your precious time dealing with the day–to–day hassles or worrying about the market.

I know that **The 3+1 Plan** works because I have thousands of clients across three countries, who have created their own **3+1 Plans** and each one works for them.

There are, of course, five traditional ways of planning for the future: pension plans; stock market portfolios; savings plans; investment in new businesses; and property.

I have been in the investment business for over fifteen years. Around the turn of the new millennium, I came to realise that three of those five ways are no longer likely to secure the financial future that you want, while the fourth requires too much luck, extreme experience, time or talent to be reliable.

Pensions, stock market investments and savings no longer bring in serious profits, and investing in new companies is too risky.

It seemed to me that only a property portfolio could achieve the successful financial future that most people rightly want. This thought led me to creating **The 3+1 Plan** and refining the strategies that would give you the wealth and lifestyle that you want.

But I know that most people still hang onto the old methods and so, before going into detail on how you can create your own **3+1 Plan,** let me look briefly at the old traditional ways.

1. Pension Plans

You might ask what's wrong with doing what millions have done in the past, which is to pay into a pension fund every month of their lives and then cash in at some time between 55 and 75 with a good income?

The sad news is that it is no longer a good income for most people. The success of your pension fund depends on two things; the state of the stock market and the efficiency of the people who are investing your money.

Unfortunately, both of these have failed. The Stock Market FT100 index is lower today than it was in the last century and at the time of writing **The 3+1 Plan,** the index is 30% down on what it was in 2000.

Secondly, most of the people managing your monthly payments have failed to earn you more than 3% p.a. on your hard-earned contributions. By an intricate system of fees, charges and dealing costs, they take over 30–40% of the money you invest with them.

The result of these two failures is that anyone cashing in on their pension in recent years has found that its value is much, much less than they hoped.

Worse is to follow. Your money, when you close your pension

fund, does not all come to you. You can't just take your money out and use it for whatever lifestyle you want to enjoy. You have to leave most of it with the insurance company.

It's true that you can take 25%, but the rest has to buy an annuity. In the nineties, your annuity could have paid you 15% a year for life; today it is only around 5%. All those years of denying yourself in order to keep up the pension payments have too often come down to a miserable payout.

But that is not all. The little money you do receive from your annuity is then taxed. You paid for your pension plan out of your net earnings, but the government then taxes you at 20 or 40%, at a time when you most need your money.

The pension game may be great for the money managers, but not for you. You give your monthly money to someone you don't know, who never tells you how things are going, and who generally takes 30% of it for their company.

The success of your investment depends on them, on the markets, on the interest rates and, even when you decide to stop throwing your money their way, they only let you have a quarter of it and use the rest to earn more fees fixing you up with an annuity.

It's madness. In fact, my view is that pensions today are one big con! In no way do they guarantee you a financially better life.

2. Savings Plans

Of course, it makes sense to save money when you have more than enough to live on and are able to put some by for the future. Savings will build an amount of capital for your future, for you to use in an emergency or when you change your lifestyle, like beginning to create your own **3+1 Plan.**

I personally used my savings as the capital to buy my first property. I had saved just under £10,000 and that was enough at that time to let me enter the magical world of property.

Sadly, although some schemes, like ISAS, are still worth doing because of the tax exemption, the return on general savings when they are taxed, is not good. Over the last decade, the interest paid on savings has often not been enough even to cover inflation. As I write this in the summer of 2009, it is difficult to find safe savings plans that pay a net 4%, while inflation on food alone is 6%.

Saving money each year is, of course, good for all of us, if only because it puts our money out of temptation's way for a year or so, but it is not going to make you rich.

3. PLAY THE STOCK MARKET

This works for some people but not for most of us. Over the last fifty years, the stock market indices show that prices doubled, on average, every ten years. In theory then, a thousand pounds put in now will be £2,000 by 2020, but this is not the record of the last decade. Prices have not doubled, but almost halved.

I don't like the stock market for two main reasons. The truth is that it is a sophisticated market which most of us do not understand, where insiders in the City are always ahead of us, and where you can buy at the wrong time and lose heavily. Most ordinary investors do not double their money; in fact they are often happy just to get their original investment back.

Just as importantly, I came to realise that playing the market takes time. It is not like it was in our parents' day: you now need to watch your shares every day and sometimes every hour.

I don't want to spend my life worrying about changes in a share price, worried that I should be buying or selling. That is not what life is about. I want an investment plan that I can set up and not have to worry about it. And so, I am sure, do you.

4. INVEST IN A BUSINESS

Potentially, this is a very enjoyable and the most profitable way of investing, if you have enough seed money to put into a business that you believe has a great future. But which companies, what product or service? Those who backed the best of the Silicon Valley IT geniuses, while they were still working out of garages, made millions, but most new companies fail and the risk for your investment is enormous.

5. PROPERTY IS THE ONLY ANSWER

As you already know by now, I believe that investing in Property is the only real answer. I believe that it is less risky than investing in new businesses, less time–consuming than investing in the stock market, more profitable than putting your money into savings, and leaves you with more of your profits than any pension scheme.

That is why it seems to me to be unarguable that a property portfolio is now the best way for you to make enough money to achieve your goal of financial security.

Let me remind you of just a few of the dozens of reasons why investing in a property portfolio makes sense to achieve your financial freedom.

The government doesn't tell you these, nor do the banks or insurance companies, or all those personal financial advisors. That's because they don't make large fees out of your money, when you invest in a few properties.

1. Building up a property portfolio is simple, not always easy, but always fun.
2. Property prices have doubled every ten years for fifty years. The British like to own property and property prices never collapse like the stock market. Even in 2009, after the fall of the last two years, those who bought at the end of the last decade are still seeing their property worth twice as much as the price they paid for it.
3. Your property portfolio is run by you, the budget is controlled by you and not handed over to some stranger to play with, who then keeps the largest part.
4. Your profits from your property portfolio are not savagely reduced by management costs, which can be 40% of the money you pay in each month into a stock market pension plan. You know exactly from your own budgets the extent of your 'management' costs.
5. The running costs of your investment properties are dramatically reduced by the income from your tenants, so that your monthly outgoings are normally far less than paying premiums into some stock market pension fund.
6. When you finally sell any of your properties, all the profit comes to you and stays with you; it's not kept from you and dribbled out to you with a few pounds each year.

But there is one point above all other points and it is unique to this form of investment. Property is all about leveraging. I don't mean to cover detail points in this Introduction, but I must remind you of the unique joy of being able to buy something with only a down payment.

When you come to create your own **3+1 Plan**, all you have to put up is the amount which a lender will not give you. It could be 10, 20, 30 or 40% depending on the market conditions, but a lender will always put up over half.

This is an extraordinary advantage. If you buy £10,000 of shares, you pay £10,000. If you put £10,000 into a savings account, you put in the whole amount. If you put £10,000 into a new company, again you put in the whole amount. If you put £10,000 into a pension plan, the government will add to it, but then grab it back at the end and tax you on your annuity.

What this power of leverage means is that you can buy, say, a £200,000 property for anything from £20,000 upwards, depending on the mortgage market at the time. The lender granting you a mortgage will pay the rest.

And, you know, there is another extraordinary benefit to you. When you decide to sell one day, the Lender doesn't want a share of your profit. You take all the profit; he just wants his loan back.

Successful investment is all about leveraging, and only property investment has that beautiful bonus.

Take an easy example. You buy a £200,000 property with a 70% mortgage. You therefore put up £60,000. Ten years down the road it doubles in value to £400,000. You have all the equity, so you can receive all £400,000 from a sale. You just pay off the loan of £140,000, and you net £260,000.

Renters have paid your interest costs to the lender and you have over four times your investment. 400% return: where else could you get that amount of profit?

Are you convinced? I hope so, but some of you may still have some concerns, because changing your future financial plans into property and away from pension plans or the stock market is a serious decision.

Before you read the rest of this book, before you begin to create **The 3+1 Plan** for yourself, I want to try to answer any concerns. I don't want you to start the book with doubts, I want you to be clear, here and now, why I am suggesting that you will find your answer in my plan.

Let's take the points one by one.

1. **I don't like being in debt.** Absolutely right, but this isn't bad debt, this is good debt. This is not a consumer debt that takes money from you; this is a debt that is paid by somebody else, in your case a tenant. This is a debt that is covered by income, not a debt that takes money from your bank balance.
2. **I wouldn't know what to buy.** You can learn that in a later chapter in **The 3+1 Plan** and how I can help.
3. **If I buy at the wrong time, my property might crash.** Of course it can, but it doesn't matter. You are making a long-term investment and the market will catch up at some point. You are not putting your money in for a quick profit; you are in for the long term.
4. **I don't know the people to look after my investment.** No, but I do. Lawyers, accountants, property managers, mortgage brokers, property managers and bankers are part of my service. Even if you don't use a service like mine, the high street is filled with people who can manage your investments for you.

5. **I don't know if I have enough money to buy another property.** You may well have it, but don't realise it. Remember that you only have to put up a small part of the total price. Remember, also, that you are planning to have your annual mortgage and running costs paid for by your rental income.

Once you start reading **The 3+1 Plan,** you will see how easily it can be done and how well it can be organised, so that you do not have anymore worries.

The rise of the buy to let market in the UK has made a property portfolio much easier to control and, although it has only been going here for a decade, it has already produced thousands of millionaires.

This confirms the remark made to me by the famous Robert Kiyosaki, of 'Rich Dad, Poor Dad' fame, that the rich may make their money from shares or businesses, but, whatever its source, they hold their wealth in property.

Is it really easy to build up a property portfolio? The truth is 'No' at the beginning, but 'Yes' once you understand this market. This is why I have written **The 3+1 Plan.**

Everything in this book is about making it easy for you to start growing your property portfolio, without the day-to-day hassles of being a full-time landlord. **The 3+1 Plan** is a very clear concept and I support that with what I call **My Set and Forget Philosophy.** This gives you the attitude and strategies to ensure that you can live your life to the full along the way, secure in the knowledge that your future (and present) is in safe hands.

This book will show you everything you need to know, so you too, can achieve **The 3+1 Plan,** while being a **Set and Forget** Property Investor. Then, all you will need to do is decide how you would most like to enjoy your time.

You will be guided through my processes, procedures, structures and strategies for developing and managing a property portfolio. I will do this by coaching you with all my knowledge and experience. I've never lost money on a property deal, but I've had some hair–raising experiences – that's where I often learned the most!

I am going to tell you a load of different stories, but I am also going to give you the basics of building a portfolio; real strategies, time–proven, not just the same old stuff on how to find the right property.

While the property is definitely important, the experienced investor doesn't ignore the strategy and structure that they use to purchase and hold the property.

One thing I ask from you. Be clear from the beginning as to your aims and objectives, so that your portfolio is created to achieve these. You should also understand that I am not talking about buying and selling for a quick return.

The 3+1 Plan is about creating a portfolio that will enable you to have enough money, ten or more years down the line, to answer those original three questions which we asked ourselves at the beginning of the introduction. Then it will be time to fulfil all your dreams.

BRETT ALEGRE-WOOD

I thought that I should add a brief note on myself, so that you had some idea about me before you begin to read **The 3+1 Plan,** and hopefully, before we meet to discuss your own **3+1 Personal Property Plan.**

I grew up in Australia, spending most of my early life in Melbourne, until my father – who was in the army – got posted to Brisbane. It was there that I spent most of my school years, until I graduated from high school and also chose a career in the military. I spent a year in the army full–time, and then enrolled in university to study international business while still in the army part–time.

It was only after leaving the army that I moved into the lucrative field of management consultancy. At a young age, I had a chance to work for many of Australia's largest companies as a consultant and I very quickly learned that a high–profile job had very little to do with financial security!

My interest in property first developed in 1994, when I trained as an estate agent with a local entrepreneur. As an estate agent I realised that although there was an abundance of people interested in purchasing property, deals would often fall through due to lack of finance.

It didn't take long before I met Peter James – one of my mentors – who was also an expert in mortgages and insurance. Peter runs one of Australia's largest non–bank lenders. He inspired me to become a mortgage broker, and soon after, I had a successful mortgage business and was training mortgage brokers across Australia. This eventually led to being accepted into the State Committee for the Mortgage Finance Association of Australia (similar to the UK's Council of Mortgage Lenders).

During this time, I began running seminars on 'How to Build Wealth through Property'. I noted that the majority of people attending my seminars were there for a similar reason: they had also come to the realisation that they couldn't rely on their pensions or their employer's plans to set them up comfortably for retirement.

On top of this, on their moderate incomes, all the scrimping and saving to put every spare penny back into the mortgage meant that what should have been the prime years of their lives were being spent slogging away at setting themselves up for a not–so–bright future.

These people believed that there must be something more out there, a better way to do it. And they were right.

During my time in Australia, I learned how to buy property and renovate it, act as a landlord and listen to endless problems that would arise from tenants. It basically just felt like I had a second stressful job and I knew that I had to organise it in a quite different way.

Since then, in the UK, Spain and three other countries around the world, I have not used a single paintbrush, hammered a nail or knocked down a single wall. I haven't dealt with sourcing tenants, or even worse, evicting them. I have bought only off plan and newly built property, each time with considerable discount and structured it in such a way as to require only minimal capital outlay.

Yes, I still have to pay my mortgages, ensure rents are received and pay the various charges, but, for the most part, my portfolio is in **Set and Forget** mode, explained fully in Chapter 2. I am free to live out my dreams and enjoy my life to the fullest, doing the things that I am passionate about.

I moved to London in 2002, initially to fulfil the typical Aussie tradition of backpacking around Europe for one or two years, while using London as a base – but I soon realised that there was a huge opportunity in property in the UK, an opportunity that still exists today.

In 2003, I published a letter to my investors explaining the current state of the property market in the UK and some of the tricks and sales tactics being used on people. This letter generated a huge amount of interest, and led me to the creation of my free *Insiders Tips & Tricks* weekly newsletter.

In 2004, interest had grown so much that I created my website, *www.YourPropertyClub.com*. Over 80,000 people now receive the newsletter and the contents of this book are the consolidated learning from all of those newsletters, combined with the practical experience of mentors, clients and my own experience.

In 2008, I married Arlene and we then bought a new home in Islington, London. In 2009, we had so many clients wanting to create their own property portfolios that I decided to begin expanding the business throughout Australia, Asia and a further five offices in the UK. I learned long ago that the time to develop your business was when others were panicking.

I also learned that a great time to build a property portfolio was when many people in the market were desperate to sell. By buying at depressed prices, you are sitting pretty when the good times return.

Welcome to the good times.

HOW DOES THE 2008/2009 CREDIT CRUNCH AND RECESSION AFFECT THIS BOOK

I would be lying if I said I forecasted the full extent of the credit crunch and recession. In fact, I have yet to find a single economic commentator who predicted what actually happened. Whether anyone did or didn't predict the eventual outcome, it actually doesn't matter. As investors, we must roll with the punches as they come.

The main changes to the mortgage market for property investors during this time were:

- Loan to values dropped from 85% down to 65%, which meant you needed extra deposit to purchase a property.
- The interest rates on buy to let shot up from around 5% to as high as 6.5%-7.5% meaning that your monthly cash flow was affected, and they then dropped again to around 5.5%.
- Most banks offered fixed rates at this higher level which meant investors were locked into cash flow shortages for two or three years.
- Rent coverage which was as low as 100% coverage raced up to 125%. This wasn't such a big deal because the loan to values had dropped sufficiently to off set this change.
- Finally, the Council for Mortgages Lenders (CML) made a number of changes, meaning that all incentives had to be declared to the lender. This limited cash backs, non–financial incentives and bridged deposit structures.

The most important thing about the lessons in this book is that some of the information may have changed by the time you read it. Interest rates may have changed, the market may have changed, loan to values may have changed, mortgage products may have changed, average prices may have gone up (or gone down). Regardless, the laws, principles, strategies and structures in the book will still apply: these won't change.

For over fifteen years and in the three different countries that I have built property portfolios, the same lessons apply, despite the criteria having changed between countries and with the different market cycles in each country.

My advice is not to get too bogged down in the current property market. It will change. Focus on the lessons and learn to apply them in any market.

You will be holding your property through a number of different property cycles and each will present different criteria and different opportunities. Becoming educated is your best defence against these changes.

Chapter 1

WHY THE 3+1 PLAN WILL WORK FOR YOU AND BECOME THE BASIS OF YOUR NEW RICHER LIFESTYLE

The **3+1 Plan** is my answer for anyone who wants to plan their finances and achieve greater wealth. It is not complicated. As you will have read in the Introduction, I believe that with three extra properties, in addition to your home, you can face the future with confidence.

The **3+1 Plan** was born out of a conversation in 1999 that I had with Peter James. We were discussing what it takes to 'practically' retire – not fully retire, necessarily, but to have the money to stop working quite as hard, take a look at your future and decide what you want to do for the next part of your life.

He argued that you only needed your own home and three other buy to let properties to get into a position to fund any retirement. At first, I thought that it seemed far too easy – only three buy to lets and your own home. So I ran the mathematics on some of my own properties and found that the numbers fitted! Actually, it worked out to be more money than if I had kept working.

I wrote about our conversation in my Financial Partners newsletter under the name '**The 3+1 Strategy**' and over the years developed it as I met with thousands of people who wanted exactly what **The 3+1 plan** offered.

Most people wanted to achieve a self–funded retirement and a supplemented lifestyle without having to spend a huge amount of their life creating this extra wealth.

I have always believed that a successful financial portfolio should be based on three things:

- You must know precisely why you are doing it.
- You must be clear about what you want and when you will want it.
- You should choose a strategy that gives you more time for living and less cause for worry.

Once you decide the first two – and only you can do those – then **The 3+1 Plan** can give you the third.

How does **The 3+1 Plan** work? There are two basic steps at the start.

STEP ONE

By the time you retire you should own your own home with no mortgage.

I was brought up to believe that 'an *Australian's home is his castle*' – in fact, we even made a hilarious comedy about it. It was called *The Castle* and it was a very funny look at the lengths that Aussies will go to to save their home.

When I moved to England I found a similar philosophy – '*an Englishman's home is his castle*' – and with around 70% of people owning their own castle, the statistics are similar to Australia.

This is why homeowners in the UK can have so much equity. They've paid off their mortgages and have seen considerable increase in the value of their homes.

It is an important part of the success of **The 3+1 Plan** that you aim to own your own home outright. Why? Two reasons.

First, because you don't want to be funding home mortgage payments at a time when you may decide to work less.

Second, because you may need to use your equity in your main property to raise money for your investment properties. Of course you will still have mortgage payments to make, but these will now be funded by your tenants, not by you.

Owning your own home is not enough anymore to achieve your dreams, but using your home to produce a new income is what many choose as one of the best ways to fund the building of their **3+1 Plan.**

Step Two

By the time you retire, you must own three Buy to Let properties.

Let's move to the **3** in **The 3+1 Plan.** The second part of the plan is to own three buy to let properties. You may ask 'Why three?' My reasoning is this.

In the UK, as in Australia, the average person spends one–third of their income on taxes, another third on living, and the final third on rent or mortgage payments.

So imagine that you have three buy to let properties, all without mortgages, so that all the rent is yours to keep. Obviously you are going to have to pay about one third in tax back to the government – which you would have to with any income – leaving you with two thirds of the rent.

You, on the other hand, don't have to pay rent or a mortgage, because you have your own home paid off in full. So the full two thirds is yours to spend as you wish. It really is that simple. Ending full–time work would not mean a savage change in lifestyle; you now have a replacement income from your **3+1 Plan.**

Let's check the numbers in case you are a bit sceptical

Assume that you earn £40,000 per year income and have bought **3+1** properties at around £200,000 each. If you were working, you would be paying around 33% tax on the £40,000 – about £13,200. You would be paying around £13,200 in rent or mortgage payments, leaving you with about £13,200 for living.

So the numbers below must get us at least £13,200 per annum in income. If you are wondering, these are three real properties in my own portfolio.

	PROPERTY 1	PROPERTY 2	PROPERTY 3	TOTAL
Value	£185,000	£210,000	£225,000	£620,000
Rent Received	£695	£750	£925	£2370
Agents Fees (10% inc VAT)	£81.66	£88.13	£108.69	£278
Net Rent in Bank	£613	£661	£816	£2090
Provision for all Costs	£80	£80	£80	£240
Net Taxable Income	£533	£581	£736	£1850
Tax on Rental Income (30%)	£159	£174	£220	£553
Remainder	£374	£407	£516	£1297

So, we have around £1,300 left over after all costs and taxes. That's £1,300 x 12 months, which is £15,600.

Let me add a little bonus to the above table. I have not even factored in the capital growth aspect. Any capital growth over and above inflation adds to your wealth.

Considering that property doubles around every 7–10 years, or about 9% annualised, you can also add at least 6% per annum on top of this. 6% of £620,000 is about £40,000 extra wealth. It doesn't take long for the numbers to add up.

So what type of properties should you buy?

You will generally buy a similar type of property that you would live in yourself. So if you live in a property worth £200,000, then you will buy properties worth around £200,000. If you earn £150,000 income, then you will probably live in a £850,000 house and buy properties around that price range instead of the £200,000 house. So it all becomes a relative game.

Now let me add another thought. This book is titled **The 3+1 Plan.** That is because I believe that this is the basis for a changed and richer life sometime down the road.

But I must be honest with you. **3+1** is fine, it works, and thousands of clients have stopped there. Equally, thousands have seen no need to stop there, but have gone on to building their portfolios, with more properties to let, more income to come in.

I will go into that later, showing how your portfolio can be built up, one by one, if that fits in with your plans.

But at the start, focus on having a small portfolio, and you will very quickly realise how easy this plan is to achieve. Once you own three properties, owning seven, ten or even fifteen, is not that much more of a step!

The simplicity of this plan means that you don't need to change jobs to achieve it, or even give up nights and weekends while you build and manage your portfolio. I am not offering you another way to spend your time making income; **I am offering a proven method to build a portfolio with very little time commitment on your part.**

Don't ever think that you'll have to invest a huge amount of extra hours running a portfolio. Keep that job you love – or if you don't love it, give it a bit of time and you'll find that your portfolio will give you the freedom to sack your existing boss and find a better one. Who knows? That new boss might be you!

I have always been a hard worker and I have always been a very passionate person; that is, as long as I am enjoying what I do and learning new things all the time. For me, **The 3+1 Plan** is not something that I would ever use to retire early; I simply use it as an emotional pillow.

You see, now that I have achieved the plan, I can rest every night in the knowledge that if I weren't enjoying what I do, I would have the freedom to choose something else. Luckily, I absolutely love what I do.

One of my clients, Martin, used to spend about 50 minutes per day driving to work in traffic and 50 minutes per day driving home from work. He started at 9 a.m. and finished at 6 p.m. meaning that he would miss taking the kids, Thomas and Anna, to school each day. Once Martin and his wife had their portfolio set up, they realised that they could change that life.

Martin approached his boss about reducing his working hours so that he could take the kids to school and pick them up each day. He would be working from 10 a.m. and finishing at 3 p.m. This would mean that it would take him 15 minutes to get to and from work and it also gave him a lot more time with the kids. Martin's quality of life increased dramatically as a result.

The best bit about the whole **3+1 Plan** is that it is indexed to inflation, so you don't have to worry about living into your hundreds! As the property's value and the rent increases over time, you will benefit from these increases, ensuring that you will continue to maintain and even enhance your fantastic lifestyle.

Initially, your investment properties will, of course, be bought with mortgages, but the final outcome is to achieve **3+1** properties with no mortgages. How can you do this? The paradoxical answer is that you buy more properties with more mortgages. I recommend to many investors that you aim at building up your portfolio to 7–10 properties, all with mortgages on them.

Madness? No. Forward planning. As the values of the properties increase, you can gradually sell some of them off and use the money to pay down the mortgages on the others. In this way you can achieve **3+1** without mortgages a lot sooner.

At what point do you pay the mortgages off? My personal opinion is simple: don't be in a hurry to pay your mortgages off; all that will do is to decrease the speed at which you can ultimately achieve **The 3+1 Plan.**

You will know when the right time is for you to pay your mortgages off, but don't be surprised if, once you are in a position to pay them off, you decide not to, preferring to keep them and letting the value of the portfolio increase while watching inflation wither away at the value of your mortgage.

Another of the joys of **The 3+1 Plan** is that the payoff time can be as flexible as you need.

Chapter 2

MY SET AND FORGET STRATEGY
SET UP YOUR PROPERTY PORTFOLIO PROPERLY AND IT WILL RUN ITSELF

My Set and Forget Philosophy is the over–riding philosophy that will help you achieve **The 3+1 Plan.** For me, the reasons that I work with property are clear: it gives me a fantastic lifestyle and allows me to help others achieve the same.

Pinning down the over–riding philosophy on which I built my portfolio – a philosophy that pervades everything I do – was a ten–year quest, until I realised that the answer was right in front of me. It can be summarised in three simple words.

SET AND FORGET

Set and Forget is more than just a strategy for your portfolio or a way you set up each of your properties. **Set and Forget** *is* the philosophy. It is present in every transaction, in every strategy. In fact, it is perhaps the most important thing I do for those who want to follow **The 3+1 Plan.**

Set and Forget is about creating efficiency in your portfolio.

I first met Murray Gray in 1994 when we worked together on a software package that allowed sales teams to become highly effi-cient. Murray was the systems expert and he was able to make my ideas become a workable system for many of Australia's top com-panies. We have worked together building portfolio–building soft-ware, systems and websites for over fifteen years now. Without his input and systemisation, as well as his ability to allow me to com-municate to the masses through the web, it would have been dif-ficult to get the portfolio–building strategies to the 'efficient' stage they are now.

Once you achieve this *efficiency* you will have time to do more of the things that you want to do, while the portfolio works itself. This is why I am so focused and passionate about **Set and Forget**.

Set and Forget, put simply, is:

Every little thing I do that has anything to do with property is set up so that I can forget it on a day–to–day basis for two years at a time; then I simply set it up again, so that I can forget it on a day–to–day basis for another two years.

So that raises three questions:

1. What do I mean by 'Set'?
2. What do I mean by 'Forget'?
3. Why do I say two years?

I will deal with each in turn, but first let me give you a practical example, in the way that I run my main current account.

- All rent is paid into my account between the 1st and 9th of the month.
- All mortgages are direct–debited out between the 1st and the 6th of the month.
- All other direct debits come out between the 1st and the 10th of the month (personal loans, TV licence, Council Tax, credit cards etc).

As you can see, between the 1st and the 10th of each month there's a lot happening in my bank account. During this period my cash flow gets Set and from the 10th onwards, I can **Forget** it because very little happens on my account. Each property becomes nothing more than a number and numbers are easy to forget. This means that I can forget the numbers and focus on living.

Simon Shankland, my business partner and director of portfolios, is a massive support in this respect. Simon worked at applying the principles in his own portfolio, as well as with our clients. His *feedback and relationship are invaluable. I first met Simon when we were drinking in an Aussie bar (The Redback Tavern) in Acton. Simon was interested in property, having grown up with his mother as an estate agent, and as he already had some property of his own in New Zealand (he's a Kiwi). That was 2004 and, in the last five years, he has built a substantial portfolio in the UK and Spain using the **Set and Forget** principles.*

You will find my full **Set and Forget Checklist** at the end of the book in Chapter 10. You can go through and see which ones you are already doing and which ones you perhaps need to put some thoughts into. As with anything, it's not a one–size–fits–all. The checklist works well for me; many of my clients do 80% of the checklist, are perfectly happy and better yet, they still make money.

1. What do I mean by 'Set'?

Setting is all about doing the little things that will save you time later and allow someone else to take responsibility for the task. I find that when most people start to build a portfolio, they uncover a massive control issue. This is something that you will have to overcome if you want to build a portfolio. In my experience, the biggest issue you will face in your portfolio is letting go of control.

My early years as a self-employed businessman are a classic case of not wanting to let go of control. I kept finding that I would get to a dozen staff or so and then the business would stagnate. I could never work out why and over time it became a little frustrating.

I guess I was about 29 when I realised that the problem was with me. I needed to let go of control, which began when I moved over to the UK and had to let go of everything into the hands of other people.

These are my portfolio managers, my mortgage brokers, my solicitors, various letting agents and a number of managing agents. I am confident that they will do their jobs and this frees up my time to do mine. It makes things so much easier when you let go of control and stop getting involved in everything.

*John and Beth signed up to my newsletter. They were successful landlords with 25 properties, and Beth worked full–time in the business. They were extremely interested in my **Set and Forget** philosophy, because they had noticed that as they built their portfolio and bought each additional property, they would spend more and more time managing it. You see, they had 25 properties, 25 tenants to manage, 25 rents to collect, 25 mortgages to pay, 25 sets of maintenance and 25 separate properties to be a full–time landlord for. They didn't know the first thing about investing, but they were awesome landlords.*

We sat down, and I very quickly identified that they needed to take back their life. They were both spending so much time on the properties dealing with issues that they didn't have a life.

*I took them through **My Set and Forget Checklist** and over the next two months we turned them from being landlords to **Set and Forget** investors. They brought on five different letting agents, who took over the management of the properties, set up the bank accounts, got them thinking about things they could be doing with all their spare time and before long they realised how great owning properties can be.*

So, Setting is about letting go of control, knowing what to let go of, and in what way, so that you can move onto the next part of the property philosophy.

2. What do I mean by 'Forget'?

If you have set your portfolio up properly, then this is the easy part. Forgetting is all about the emotions. You have to realise that until you build your emotional intelligence as an investor, you will find it hard to forget, but, as time goes on, you will grow to appreciate the fact that someone else is doing all the work for you.

Just wait until your first remortgage: it might only be for £20,000, but when you add the actual hours you worked on that property, you will wonder why you didn't start years ago.

Now please don't think that you will ever completely forget a property or have no emotional response at all. As humans, we live emotionally expressive lives, but with emotional intelligence you can control these responses through a combination of education and experience. My aim with this book is to help you with both.

3. Why do I say Two Years?

Property is a slow–moving wealth vehicle, unlike investing in the stock market or owning a business, which can change in an instant. The property market moves gently forward, with the occasional pause and perhaps a few steps back, but upwards for most of the time. The important thing to remember is that everything happens slowly.

This means that if you set up correctly, it will be a long time before the market has changed enough that you need to reset your portfolio. It gives you plenty of time to ponder decisions, change decisions and generally move with the market.

This is why I look at things in two–year portions. The plan is to hold the property for the long-term and, by breaking it down into two–year portions, make it very easy to manage and forget.

I am not saying that you totally forget your portfolio for a full two years. I am simply saying that if you plan to have your portfolio in **Set and Forget** mode for two years, that will allow the property enough time to gain in value.

Paul bought a property and found a tenant through a local letting agent. The mortgage he chose was a two-year fixed rate, and the tenant signed a twelve-month assured short hold tenancy agreement. His total shortfall was £190 per month so he put aside two years' worth of money into a separate provision account. His agent is fully managing the property and they will deduct anything up to £300 in maintenance direct from the rent received. For anything over this, they will call him. Paul's service charge is paid by monthly direct debit and his ground rent is paid every six months by cheque. It was a new apartment, so there shouldn't have been any maintenance or other problems, but just in case, he had a snagging inspector deal with any problems with the property and have them fixed.

Realistically, the only time you should hear from the property manager is when the tenant hands in their one–month notice (in which case you will immediately instruct the agent to find a new tenant and assess the possibility of raising the rent). The only other event you have to consider is if, during one of his regular reviews, he notices that property prices or rents are rising dramatically.

On a monthly basis, all you need to do is ensure that the agent has deposited the rent into your account and that the mortgage payment has come out of the bank. Once every six months you need to write a cheque for the ground rent which you have already provided for in the £190 per month, so you don't need to scramble for the money.

This property is truly in **Set and Forget** mode for the next two years. Count up the hours of your time it takes to do all this, and you will be surprised how little actual time you spend on this property.

You really don't have to know much about the state of the local property market, because the only time you need to consider your property, or where the market is at, is once every two years when you want to restructure it.

But you do have to know when all your properties need your attention, and that is why I created a piece of software in 2000 to record the details of all my properties. It is now yours to use free.

EzyTrac Portfolio Management System

At the heart of my **Set and Forget** philosophy is **EzyTrac**. It started as a basic spreadsheet to record the details of my properties and grew into a mammoth seven worksheet programme. In late 2003 I began using **EzyTrac** with clients. The problem was that every time I made a change to the formulas on the spreadsheet, I had to change every client's formulas. For this reason I have had the program written into my company website.

You can access EzyTrac free at: *www.ezytracproperty.com*

The bigger your portfolio, the more difficult it may be to manage. This is when you will benefit from a bit of assistance to track rents, ground rents, service charges, tenancy expirations and mortgage payments. You can track all of the basics with this, and watch your portfolio grow. One of my favourite and most useful functions is that it allows you to see and record important dates and have an e-mail reminder sent.

This software is definitely recommended to anyone who has more than three properties. It will give you total peace of mind and allow you to manage the growth of your portfolio, ensuring that you will always have enough cash flow, as well as reminding you to remortgage or sell with plenty of time to spare.

It will also allow you to look up to ten years into the future and track the growth of your portfolio. This is like a radar, in that it can help predict future potential problems. Basically, it will help you pass the sleep test on almost any property or portfolio.

Set and Forget mastery

As with anything at the start, **Set and Forget** begins with faith and over time will develop into certainty. I have reached a level of certainty where my emotional response to any situation is quite numb or downright non-existent. Once you get to this level, you have truly mastered the **Set and Forget** philosophy.

I began developing the **Set and Forget** principles in Australia, in the form of my Financial Partners newsletters. At that stage, e-mail barely existed, so I would colour-print it every month with tips and tricks on investing. At the time, it was more of a great way for my team to stay in contact with their clients.

Who would have thought that over one decade later, it would consist of hundreds of articles, a book, nine booklets, twenty-seven websites, countless success stories and thousands of properties sold in the UK, Spain and Australia?

I think the thing that appealed to me initially about **Set and Forget** was the fact that I was too busy with building my business in Australia to put time into my portfolio.

I remember having a tenant who didn't pay the rent for over three months. I was so busy that I hadn't even noticed. When I contacted the tenant it turned out that they had moved out about a month earlier. It's funny how some of our biggest lessons come out of our biggest mistakes.

My property mentors, Peter and Alec, were a big influence in the development of these principles. Peter gave me a practical view of property and all its facets. Alec gave me a 'hard–nosed' investor attitude to property. Both were great men in their own rights and helped the development of these principles. Then in later years, it was the feedback from clients that really built on the foundations.

The **Set and Forget** strategies evolve with each new experience, but the fundamentals remain the same. Investing in property is not some abstract investment project. **The 3+1 Plan is about achieving wealth, alongside an enhanced life.**

Chapter 3

HOW DO YOU RAISE THE CAPITAL REQUIRED?
IT'S EASIER THAN YOU THINK

Ok, so let's start looking at money. I constantly write about structure and strategy, and structure is initially based on the most effective use of your capital.

When I speak to new clients, I always put them through a brief qualification process before deciding to work with them. One of the criteria is, *'Do you have at least £25,000 of capital to invest?'*

I am very cautious of working with people who have less than £25,000. Consider for a moment two people who are starting out investing. One has £25,000 and the other £250,000. An opportunity comes along and requires £25,000. They both decide to take advantage. The investor with £25,000 has to invest 100% of their capital, or, to put it another way, 100% of their total financial net worth. The investor with £250,000 invests only 10% of their total funds. Let me ask you this: 'Who is going to be more emotional?' Clearly, it's the first.

One of the problems I face all the time is people who call me up for portfolio advice who have bought 'no money–down deals'. Hilary and Peter were such clients. I had spoken to them two years earlier about starting their portfolio, but they didn't have enough available equity for me to help them. They started anyway with another investment company. About two years later, they had a wonderful portfolio of seven properties. 'Well done,' you may say.

Well, not quite. Hilary and Peter bought them all with no money down and even some with cash–backs. This is when, after completion, you will receive some money back from the developer or investment company. This sounded great and they bought them with 90% mortgages on all. Their shortfalls on the seven properties were about £1,600 per month after all costs.

Oh! I forgot to tell you that the previous two years had used up all of their equity and cash–backs and, when they contacted the bank to draw some money out, they were told the rents were no-where near covering them and it was not possible. The mortgages were one-by-one going onto standard variable rate, which further worsened their cash flow. It had got to the point where they couldn't afford the shortfall and had no chance of remortgaging.

The final nail in the coffin was that the original 15% 'instant' equity they were sold was actually turning out to be a 5% negative equity. Selling was out of the question. So much for their no–money–down purchases.

I often find that people with little or no equity are the ones that have unrealistic expectations. They want unachievable results in ridiculous timelines. I am not saying that you cannot build a portfolio unless you have capital. What I am saying is that, if you don't have a large amount of capital, you are going to need to understand the market and to have discipline.

I believe discipline is something that is more important than capital. If I were asked the one characteristic that separates success from failure, rich from poor, it would be discipline. Discipline over all else.

Ever since I have trained myself to be disciplined, to honour my commitments in a disciplined way, I have seen my results amplified. Without absolute discipline you will see your capital dwindle very quickly. 'A fool and their money are soon parted.'

Discipline means doing what you say you will do, not compromising, sticking to your strategy, taking it that extra mile. It encompasses so many aspects of property. In particular, if you haven't worked out how you will secure the capital to begin building a portfolio, this chapter has ideas that can help. But before we get into that you need to understand a bit about structure.

I always say that the spectrum of structures when purchasing a property runs from the white through the grey and into the black.

The **white** is how the average investor buys property. It's probably how you bought your first property and for most people it is the only way they will ever buy property. It follows the law by the strictest guidelines and benefits all the other parties in the deal. The white is structured in the banks' and mortgage lenders' favour, which means that when using these structures, you have to use a heap of capital on each purchase.

The **black** is illegal and although you certainly don't want to be here, the unfortunate fact is that some investors do end up here when working with inexperienced, unprofessional or downright unethical property companies and agents.

The **grey** is where I like to play.

It's where the *highly* educated investor plays. It is perfectly legal, even though most people would proclaim that *you can't do that!* Unlike the white, the odds are definitely in your favour. The trouble with operating in the grey is that it changes so often.

You must keep up to date with the latest changes in the market, lending criteria and, most importantly, legislation. If you don't, what was grey when you started can turn out black before you complete!

This is one of the reasons why I love newly built ('stock') properties. The grey structure you choose when you reserve is the same structure you complete the property on and, as you'll hear me say many times, *I like certainty!*

RAISING THE CAPITAL

There are four ways to raise capital and, in building your port-folio I suggest that you should have a detailed understanding of all four. These are:

1. **Using your savings**
2. **Using existing equity by remortgaging**
3. **Borrowing from friends and family**
4. **Borrowing from other places**

1. YOUR SAVINGS

Whilst there are many ways in which you can raise capital to begin investing, I always suggest that you need to start off with some plain old–fashioned disciplined saving. This will build the necessary habits that are required to pay a mortgage.

I have to tell you that I began my career in property with the savings I had invested every month. It gave me my first capital to put down on my first property investment. Saving regularly is not only an important discipline, but can quickly be turned into capital and allow you to begin your own **3+1 Plan.**

The most efficient way to save in the UK is through an ISA. Each UK resident has the right to save money in a tax free Investment Savings Account, and from 2009 you can save up to a maximum of £10,200 per year. So the first year that you do this you have £10,200 tax–free; the following year you'll be able to add another £10,200, and so forth. This is the best way to save money tax–free, and it's my first choice for a savings account.

The problem with saving

Lots of people feel they cannot afford to save money, that there just isn't enough left at the end of the month to put away for the future. I have worked with hundreds of people over the past decade, who have said the same thing.

My answer is always the same – 10/20/70: 10% of your net income for the future, 20% for the past and 70% for the present.

- **10% for the future** – This means that as soon as you receive your wage each month, immediately take out 10% and put it aside for the future. This has to be in a separate investment account.
- **20% for the past** – This is the money you use to pay your debts off.
- **70% for the present** – This is what's left over. Once you have put aside your 10% for the future and paid your 20% on past debts, the rest is guilt free spending.

3rd Taxes

Don't worry, **10/20/70** will feel awkward and even impossible for about three months, then you will wonder why you didn't do it so long before. Again, discipline is the key to achieve this.

I remember my close mate back in Australia, Jenny, who complained of never having any money. So I put her on the program. She cleared around $2,000 per month and had around $5,000 in debts that she'd had 'all her life!' The fact was that she was constantly stressed because she owed money. Her sole financial focus was on debt.

I put her on the 10/20/70 program, and to her credit she followed it to the letter. In three months we had a review and the difference was amazing. I asked how she felt. 'Fantastic, I have $600 in my investment account now,' she replied. The smile radiated from her face, the stress was gone and her face showed a woman on a mission.

*The simple power of this is that, when all she had was $5,000 in debt, that's all she could focus on. I simply gave her something else to focus her attention on, **increasing** savings by $200 per month. She didn't have to worry about her debts because the 20% or $400 was going toward them. As they were looked after, this allowed her to see her growing pot of gold.*

You see, I have many millions of pounds in mortgages which some may call debt, but I only focus on the equity bit. So I never really worry about the mortgages as long as I have the equity.

I remember sitting down with Chloe, who worked with Simon and me for a few years. She wanted to buy a house, but didn't have the required deposit saved. We put her on the 10/20/70 plan and to her credit she completed on her first property in 2008 on her 24th birthday.

Focused payment plan for debt reduction

If you are worried about having some debt, and want to get rid of it as quickly as you can, then I have a debt reduction technique that I learned many years ago which has helped hundreds of people reduce debt and gain control of their money.

The simple premise of focus payments is that you focus as much of your payments on one debt, whilst paying the minimum on all the others.

Let's take a look at the process:

1. Draw up a table listing all of your debts and complete all of the columns as in the next table.

Debt	Balance Owing	Interest Rate	Min Monthly Payment	Factor (Balance Owing/Min Mthly Payment)	Paying off order
Cuddle Personal Loan	£8,712	6.9%	£257	33.9	Third
SA Mortgage	£150,000	5.75%	£718	208.9	Last
National Credit Card	£5,000	12.8%	£136	36.8	Fourth
XYZ Credit Card	£3,000	19%	£138	21.7	First
Smile Personal Loan	£2,000	9.9%	£91	22	Second

2. In the factor column you simply take the total balance owing and divide it by the minimum monthly repayment. This will give you a factor. So in this example the Cuddle Personal loan would be £8,712 divided by £257 so the factor will be 33.9.

3. Next place them in order from lowest factor through to highest factor.

4. Use your 20% for the past to make only the minimum payments on each debt except the lowest factor debt that all your additional payments will be *focused* on.

Let's say that you have a maximum of £1,700 per month that can be used to fulfil all your financial commitments. With focus payments you would make all the minimum payments on your credit cards, personal loans and mortgages come to £1,340 per month. So you have an extra £360 per month that can be applied to debt reduction.

Practically, this will mean that you will choose the xyz credit card and make a payment each month of £498 (£360 + £138). This should have it paid off within the next seven months, once you consider interest over that period. You would then focus your payments on the Smile Personal Loan with £589

(£498 + £91). You would have this paid off in five months once you have considered interest.

The Cuddle Personal loan is next, with £846 per month. This will be paid within the next 12 months. So you'll then focus on the National Credit Card with £982 repayments per month – so in three months it will be gone. You can then focus a massive £1,700 on the mortgage. This would reduce the term of your mortgage by a huge amount.

The obvious condition of this is that you don't get into more debt, so I recommend cutting up most of your cards. I say most, because at certain periods, they are useful as a means of raising capital in the short term.

Credit card companies love us, because we pay literally billions of pounds per year in interest from their plastic, but it doesn't have to be that way.

In order to get us to become customers they make offers of 0% interest for a year or so and sometimes throw in a low interest rate until the whole amount is paid off. When you need capital look at these offers on the financial websites; you may find part of your capital there.

I am not saying that credit cards should ever be your main source of capital, but I do have clients who have taken advantage of the special offers to raise the extra £5–10,000 that they needed, and they have done so at an interest rate fixed until they pay off the loan.

2: Using Existing Equity

The second and preferable way to raise capital is to remortgage or release equity from your current portfolio. It basically works like this:

Valuation: £100,000
Maximum loan: 85% or £85,000
Current mortgage amount: £60,000
£85,000 minus £60,000 leaves us with £25,000 available equity that is released and used to build your portfolio.

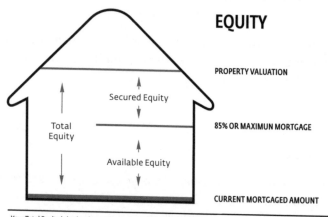

Your Total Equity is broken in two types - Secured Equity which the funder holds as their security and Available Equity which you are potentially free to use build your portfolio.

The above calculations assume firstly that you are able to borrow this much and secondly that you can service this much debt.

3: Parents and Co-ownership

This is becoming a more and more popular part of the test. Many people are now looking to parents to supply the necessary capital to begin investing. First-time buyers are also looking at co-ownership with friends.

In my experience, both these are fraught with potential problems, so my only recommendation is to make sure that, before you purchase the property, you complete a Joint Ownership Agreement. This is a legally binding document that outlines what happens if someone wants to sell the property, remortgage the property or transact the property in any way. It will also clearly outline the percentages of ownership.

I have been in property for long enough to see many occasions when a Joint Ownership Agreement would have saved a lot of pain and family drama.

4: Borrowing

Yes that's right: take a personal loan or use a credit card to get started. You will of course, have to factor in your repayments on the loans as well as your mortgage.

Should you use credit cards, overdrafts and personal loans to build your portfolio?

One of the great things about building a portfolio in the UK is that you are not confined to your income and the rent you receive to fund your portfolio. You have access to any number of sources of capital, including credit cards, overdrafts and personal loans that will give you up to £25,000 unsecured or more if you secure it against one of your existing properties.

Before I continue, let me say that I am not a big fan of consumer-related debt, nor do I think that using high-interest rate debt is necessarily a good idea. However, if you are building a portfolio then you have the choice to employ any and all means to build that portfolio. Credit cards and personal loans are one way to do this – as long as you manage it without worry.

Debt is a dirty word

As a society we attach so much negative emotion to this word 'debt.' So the first thing I do is drop the word and replace it with 'capital'. *Successful people use capital to build wealth.*

The only difference between this borrowed capital and cash is that this capital will affect your cash flow in the form of additional repayments.

Even if you borrow £25,000 for your portfolio, you can only invest about £15,000 of it, as the other £10,000 is needed for costs on the investment property and for repaying the debt on the mortgage for the following two years.

Make no mistake, it is a much higher-risk strategy than other ones, but as always the rewards can be greater. Always remember that you have to pay it back. It's so important to run the numbers upfront in order to stay on top of the cash flow.

I once had a client who borrowed £25,000 on an unsecured personal loan and then told me he had £25,000 in cash (no borrowings). He bought a property from me that had a cash flow shortfall of about £150 per month. So add to that shortfall the loan repayments of £400 per month and you have a huge shortfall of £550 per month for a single property. I don't need to tell you the added emotional strain of borrowing.

Using a gifted deposit to minimise your deposit

One of the easiest ways to minimise the amount of money you need to put into each deal is the use of a gifted deposit.

This is one of the benefits you get in buying a new build or off plan property direct from a developer: the ability to use a gifted deposit, builder's incentive or a builder's gift. They allow you to put less money into the deal by using all or part of the discount that you have, I hope, negotiated toward the normal deposit that you would require which we'll discuss later on.

A builder's gift works like this. Under a normal £100,000 deal, you would put in 15% plus costs of say 5%. So let's say £20,000 would be required to purchase the buy to let property.

If you used a gifted deposit of say 5%, you would only be required to pay a deposit of 10% plus costs so your total outlay would be £15,000 or £5,000 less than not using a gifted deposit.

Practically, all that happens with a gifted deposit is that at completion, when the developer's solicitor accepts the funds for completion, they simply reduce this amount by the amount of the gift. That's why it's called a builder's gift.

They definitely serve a great purpose and many of my clients have used them to decrease their initial acquisition costs.

The bridge – remortgage structure

This quite advanced structure requires two distinct stages to complete the structure. The first involves buying the property at a discount (or below market value) and using a bridging product such as a short–term mortgage. The second part involves a remortgage on the property that pays out the bridge and sets you up in a standard mortgage product.

Let's take a look. Imagine a property valued at £100,000 that you are buying at £90,000. You apply for a bridging mortgage product at 85% of the £90,000 or £76,500. On completion, you need to pay the remaining deposit of £90,000 minus £76,500, that's £13,500 plus costs for completion.

At the same time, you apply to do a remortgage to 85% of £100,000 or £85,000.

Once the remortgage takes place you will receive back the difference between £85,000 and £76,500 or £8,500.

BRIDGE	REMORTGAGER
Contract Price - £90,000	New Valuation - £100,000
Mortgage @ 85% - £76,500	Mortgage @ 85% - £85,000
Deposit required - £13,500	From Remortgage - £8,500

Actual deposit is only £13,500 minus £8,500 or £5,000

Buying the property at the lower price you can immediately remortgage at the higher price withdrawing your capital

A couple of points to note:
- The remortgage can be completed on the same day as completion, or it can be completed at some stage after completion. Bridging mortgage products normally charge between 1% and 3% for up to 30 days. This means you must complete the remortgage within 30 days or you will be charged another fee.
- The most important consideration when getting a bridge remortgage is that you must get a valuation at the full value of £100,000, as without it the remortgage won't take place.
- You need to remember that most standard mortgage products will not allow a remortgage to take place within six months of

completion, so you won't be able to use the mortgage company of your choice all the time.

Ok, let's change the pace a bit and look at the concept of leverage, the most important word in property.

THE TWO MOST IMPORTANT CONCEPTS IN CREATING WEALTH: OPT AND OPM

I have always remembered these two acronyms and have applied them with great success in my life. They are the two ways to amplify your results in anything in life, including your portfolio.

OPT (Other People's Time)

My Set and Forget Philosophy is all about giving other people the tasks, using their time to amplify the results of my time. This is fundamental to your success because we all have only 24 hours a day.

John from Hamble Accommodation has looked after one of my properties since 2004. In that time I have not had to visit the property once. All I have needed to do is speak to his team maybe five times and respond to ten or so e-mails. Yet in the five years he has managed the property, I have had five different tenants, a mould problem, a rubbish problem, a dirty carpet problem, a washing machine problem, a flood, a tenant cancel the tenancy and leave early as well.

I had no idea these things had happened until after they were solved and I received my rent receipt summary in the mail. John and his team sorted everything out for me without a single thought on my part. That's what I love about employing other people's time.

OPM (Other People's Money)

This is the most fundamental principle in property. It is the biggest reason why I choose property over any other asset class. On every property, I can get a mortgage that turns every £1,500 into £10,000 through using other people's money.

Consider this. I have £1,000 to invest, which makes me 10% in a year. So at the end of the year I have £1,100 or £100 return on my investment. Using OPM I borrow an extra £9,000 so I have £10,000 to invest and make the same 10%. I now have £11,000 minus interest costs in borrowing of £500. In this example, I made an extra £400 because I borrowed the extra money.

I am a big believer that, so long as you carefully consider and track your cash flow, then it is better to borrow the maximum mortgage available than to limit the amount of your mortgage, so that the property is cash flow positive.

Let me qualify that. As long as you track your cash flow, it is better to borrow the maximum mortgage rather than limiting it to being cash flow positive.

If you have an established portfolio, this may not be the case, but as you are applying **The 3+1 Plan** your capital is so important that you want to put the minimum into each property.

Let's take a look at a real–life choice that I had to make about how to fund three of my properties.

OPM LEVERAGE

NO LEVERAGE	LEVERAGE
Investment £1,000	£1,000 Own money £9,000 Borrowed OPM £10,000 Total investment
10% return / 12 months	£11,000 £9,450 Less loan / interest (5%)
£1,100 Own money	£1,550 Own money

You are £450 better off at the end of the period.

Using the leverage of other people's money means you can
maximise your returns on every deal.

OPTION 1: Borrow less – cash flow neutral

PROPERTY 1
Purchase price: £189,950
Mortgage for neutral: £123,820
Loan to Value Mortgage: 65%
Input on Completion: £38,295

This will allow you to make a big enough surplus each month to pay for the expenses every month making the cash flow exactly neutral. This will change if interest rates change.

PROPERTY 2
Purchase price: £169,950
Mortgage for neutral: £110,112
Loan to Value Mortgage: 65%
Input on completion: £30,946

PROPERTY 3
Purchase price: £182,500
Mortgage for neutral: £149,888
Loan to Value Mortgage: 82%
Input on Completion: £7,062

Total input on completion for three properties – £76,303

OPTION 2: Borrow more – cash flow negative each month

Using the same properties as above, and applying for 85% mortgages for each property, your total input, given my Two-Year Cash Flow Rule (discussed in the next chapter) would be £19,077. Consider this as the figure you would need to put away for the three properties to last you a full two years.

The difference between the two options is £57,225.

If you are concerned that property values won't rise in two years, then consider three years, which would be £28,616 or five years at £47,693. I think you would agree that after five years, the property would have increased in value enough to remortgage it and the rents would also have gone up enough to do that. This is still less than the £76,000 you were planning on putting in initially.

You could actually have a full cash flow for eight years for the same money. Surely you would agree that after eight years the property would be ripe for remortgage or selling and you would have made huge money in appreciation.

Achieving the maximum leverage is very important if you want to buy more properties, but let's suppose you are only thinking about a single property and how you are going to make money out of it. We'll start with an extreme case. It's the worst performing property in my portfolio in terms of cash flow.

I have a property in Newcastle city centre, which in 2007 needed a whopping £412 per month. Yes, every month it cost me £412 out of my pocket. So how do I make this property work?

Imagine this cost to me: £412 per month x 2 years = £9,888, or, if we look over ten years, it becomes £49,440. So the cash flow side of this property is not looking too hot at the moment.

Let's look from a capital appreciation perspective. The property is currently worth £265,000. If we assume that it doubles over the next ten years it will be worth £265,000 x 2 = £530,000. Not a bad little earner for ten years.

So if I take the £265,000 increase in capital minus the cash flow it costs to hold onto the property, £265,000 – £49,440 = £215,560. So in ten years I have made over £200,000 clear funds.

But it doesn't end there. Over that period I have been able to refinance the property, purchase other properties and do the same on these.

Here are a couple of things that we haven't considered. I have assumed that interest rates will remain the same rate throughout the ten years. This is highly unlikely. I have also assumed that the rent I will receive has never increased. This is also unlikely, and in fact the property is now cash flow negative by only £57 a month.

The final thing to consider is this:

I only paid £209,780 for the property and, because it actually had a 17% discount, I didn't have to put any money down. The only costs were £5,000 for furniture because I initially bought it as a corporate let.

All in all, I have put down £5,000, then £412 per month for ten years and made £200,000 plus.

There are obviously massive assumptions made in these figures, but the principle holds true. Sometimes what seems a really bad cash flow investment will actually turn into a good one if you hold it long enough – assuming you can afford the £412 per month.

One of the biggest lessons you can learn in property is that the real money in property is in the holding.

I remember a chat I had with Peter: he told me the story of a property that he bought and sold and made x amount of money on. He said he regretted selling it because about five years after selling it, he found out how much more it was worth. He stopped, turned to me and said 'Don't worry, at some point you will learn the same lesson the hard way!' I replied 'No mate, why would I ever sell a property?'

I sold my home on the Gold Coast in Australia in 2002 for $580,000 having seen its value more than double over the previous three years. I thought I had a great deal. Well I am happy to say that Peter was right. In about 2006, the property was worth about $1.1 million. I learned the lesson well and since that day, I am happy to say I have not sold a single property.

Once again, the real money in property is in the holding.

Chapter 4

WATCH YOUR CASH FLOW
IT'S OFTEN MORE IMPORTANT
THAN YOUR CAPITAL

Before I go into the detail of the property dynamics of capital, it's important to understand there are two dynamics of property investment. I say dynamics because they are constantly changing and interacting with each other. Having too little or too much of one can affect the other.

- **Capital growth**
- **Cash flow**

There are two primary reasons that we buy property. The first is for capital growth and this is essential, so that as inflation degrades the value of our investments, the capital growth will ensure that they remain equal or above the rate of inflation (traditionally property has done this). The second is to create a cash flow to fund our lifestyles.

Both reasons are important, but managing the two apparently opposing dynamics can become an art if you wish to achieve **The 3+1 Plan.**

Cash flow refers to the monies that you receive in rent, and the outgoings that you have to pay in the form of mortgage payments, maintenance, insurances and things such as ground rent and service charges.

The mistake that some people make is that they see cash flow as just income or rent. You must consider both the inputs (rent) and outputs (expenses and costs).

It's the interaction between cash flow and capital that is most important when growing a portfolio. How cash flow and capital interact with each other will change between properties, areas, the economic cycle, mortgage products available and many other factors.

But irrespective of the market, cash flow is the most important thing to watch.

No bank ever repossessed a property because of negative equity. They have, however, repossessed thousands of properties that were not cash flowed. It's for this reason that it's vital that you know how your cash is flowing - mortgage payments, expenses, shortfalls, everything.

It only takes one missed mortgage payment to stuff up your credit rating and stop all chance of achieving The 3+1 Plan (or at least delaying it).

We want to look at holding property indefinitely, or, I normally say, for 7–10 years. So one option for our cash flow would be to put aside a full ten years of cash flow upfront: this way we could truly **Set and Forget** the property. The problem is, who really has that much capital sitting around with no purpose? Not many, so obviously we have to find a comfortable middle–ground.

In my experience, putting aside a full two years of cash flow for every property is more than enough. It is so important that I call it a rule!

My 2 Year Cash Flow Rule

The 2 Year Cash Flow Rule is one of the best aspects of **My Set and Forget Philosophy** and an essential tool for building a successful property portfolio.

It's a simple concept that some people often forget to think about before committing to buying a property. In most cases, these people work out only the initial acquisition costs and as long as they have the funds required to purchase it, they will dive head–first into purchasing hoping to sort it all out later.

In addition – and even worse – although some of these people will consider the monthly mortgage, they'll neglect things like service charges, ground rent and, most importantly, fluctuations in interest rates.

Capital growth will make you money, but not having capital growth is at worst, a frustration. You see, the real issue to pay attention to is having sufficient cash flow to pay the mortgage, whatever the interest rate.

I have a client who needed to find an extra £1,200 a month each and every time rates went up by just 0.25%. You can imagine how much that would have hurt if he hadn't made allowances before-hand.

Some other clients of mine, Theresa and Ngozi, bought three properties through my company spending all of the capital they had allocated to purchasing property during our first meeting. Now, although they used all their capital for buying property, they still had a provision of over £60,000, which was for the various 2 Year Cash Flows from each property, as well as some money to buy a second family car.

But after three properties they had caught the property bug. That's the bug you get once you realise that the emotional side of invest-ing doesn't rule you anymore and all you want to do is buy more property. So they jumped on the phone wanting to buy another property.

*This is the danger – if I had allowed them to proceed, they would potentially have been short on their **2 Year Cash Flow** and maybe in one year's time, they would be feeling the strain on their cash flow. As it stood they took my advice and held off investing further at that stage. Two years on, they are in an awesome position with their portfolio.*

How long should you consider cash flow?

As I have stated, and will go on stating in this book, the answer is two years.

This is simply because a lot happens in property in two years! Property prices can go up and come down, interest rates can go up and come down, and the market will change. If you have a new property, two years will give the property plenty of time to settle into its surroundings and ensure a stable rental market is established.

After two years, you should safely be able to refinance, sell or at least have the flexibility to make changes that will enable you to recalculate and allow for your projected cash flow for a further two years.

When I explain **My 2 Year Cash Flow Rule** to clients, they usually ask one of three questions:

1. Is two years too short?

If you track the property market, you'll find that the only time that two years may fall short from a cash flow perspective is in times of high interest rates, when the rental coverage won't allow you to remortgage, or in times when the property market is sluggish or dropping. In the majority of cases, we can work out (approximately) how high interest rates are heading and simply adjust our cash flow accordingly. Don't worry, I'll show you my Mortgage Cost Averaging Principle later that will help.

2. Is two years too long?

The only time two years is too long is when property prices are galloping upward. In this case, you will normally be able to refinance or remortgage within two years and take some money out but you'll need to put some effort into calculating the ongoing cash flow of the property, so you can be fully prepared for whatever the market may throw at you.

I had a place in London that I bought in 2003. It was off plan and increased in value by about £50,000 by the time it completed in 2004. I immediately remortgaged and took out my initial deposit of £30,000. So at this stage, it had cost me nothing to buy. About six months later, the property increased by another £30,000, so I arranged a further advance and took out £20,000. I didn't look at the property again until the middle of 2006, at which time I was able to take a further £80,000 out of the property. So even though it's a 2 Year Cash Flow, that doesn't mean that you cannot review the portfolio much more regularly.

3. What do we do when our 2 Year Cash Flow is up?

Don't forget that the **2 Year Cash Flow** is just like an insurance policy for your properties against what we call the Realistic Worse Case Scenario (RWCS). You're essentially putting money aside for things that just don't end up happening. In most cases, the amount you're setting aside might last for 3 or even 4 years.

Let's take an example.

You have £100,000 in available equity that you can borrow from your home mortgage. You have a flexible mortgage in place and are ready to spend it. We work out that, if tomorrow you spend the entire £100,000 at 6%, it would cost you £500 per month in interest payments or £12,000 over two years. So we promptly set aside £12,000 to fund the fact those payments on the home for the next two years. This leaves us with £88,000 to invest.

So let's say that it takes us two months to buy our first property. This has immediately saved us £500 x 2 months on interest or extended our cash flow out by another two months. So we have 26 months of cash flow secured.

If you do the **2 Year Cash Flow Rule** on this first property, it comes out that we need £15,000 to purchase the property and another £5,000 for cash flow for the two years. The £5,000 we are putting aside now works the same as the £12,000 on our home. We only spend a little bit each month, but we act as if we spent it all on the first day after completion. So we are saving interest.

Just because we are measuring everything in two year periods doesn't mean that I am saying you should remortgage every two years. You will regularly review your portfolios progress and make decisions based on that review.

Nor does it mean that you should take as much money as possible out whenever you can. You simply make a decision based on emotions, cash flows, stage of the property market, capital remaining and a host of other factors discussed in this book.

The 2 Year Cash Flow Rule does NOT mean you have to remortgage every two years – only that you view each property over a two year period and make decisions based on that period.

How do you accurately calculate your cash flow?

The main lesson I have learned is to understate income and overstate expenses. This is one that I learned very early on, when I first started running a 'spending plan'. A spending plan is like a budget, except that rather than focusing on the negative side of budgeting a spending plan provides for everything you need, and then whatever is left is yours to spend. It's a lot more motivational than a budget.

The principle is that the more you build your portfolio, the more you should overstate your expenses and understate your expected income. This will simply result in more 'meat on the bone' or security in your portfolio. 'Meat on the bone' is a saying that means 'You don't spend every last penny, you don't remortgage every last pound, you leave some money behind'.

I am not suggesting that you do this when it comes to your tax situation, as you'll end up in hot water, but by consciously overstating expenses and understating income, you will have cash flow left over.

There are three factors to take into account when calculating your cash flow:

1. **Your income**
2. **The property's income (after expenses)**
3. **The principle of trading capital for cash flow**

1. Your Income

At the heart of **My Set and Forget Philosophy** of portfolio management is my belief that *you should spend your income and let me spend your capital*. Now, before you think that I am suggesting that I or anyone runs off with your capital, let me explain.

In order to build a property portfolio, you are going to need to put aside some capital to get started. Once you have allocated this capital you shouldn't need to sacrifice your lifestyle on top of this capital to build the portfolio. You should only ever enhance it.

So whether it's me that supports you to spend your capital or any other third party, the point is that you shouldn't constantly have to take lifestyle cuts to fund your portfolio. Once you have set aside an amount of capital, work within this capital to build your portfolio.

Mary and Matt were on a tight budget with two kids and only Matt's income to survive on. Nonetheless, they managed to buy their home and built considerable equity in it. So once we had remortgaged and set it up, we had to make sure that the £80,000 that they had set up from a remortgage was enough to both buy and hold their portfolio for the long term. To expect Matt's income to supplement the portfolio would have crippled them.

Naturally, this rule assumes that you have equity available to invest. If you don't, then you'll need to use your income to create capital. I am a great believer that most people can build their portfolio within the confines of their present lifestyle, meaning they won't have to sacrifice their present lifestyle to build a property portfolio.

Remember:
Building a portfolio should give you more enjoyment of life, not less.

2. THE PROPERTY'S INCOME

The second element of cash flow is the creation of a difference between the rent you receive and the expenses you pay out. In the UK it is less and less likely that you will have a cash flow positive property unless you are buying a low–value property.

The basic point is this: **your portfolio is unlikely to fund itself from the beginning**. To do that, you would need to put a massive deposit on each property, which would burn up capital very quickly limiting the size and speed of growth of your portfolio.

3. FUNDING CASH FLOW USING CAPITAL

So unless you want to slow the rate of growth of your portfolio or take the ultra–conservative route, I suggest that you become accustomed to funding any cash flow shortfalls with the capital profits you make.

Jay and Preeti had a monthly portfolio shortfall of £100 per month. So in the short term, they needed to fund this £100 per month out of their existing capital or cash flow. In their case they remortgaged their property and pulled out £20,000 through a remortgage.

So they put away the cash flow shortage of £100 per month for 24 months or £2,400, funded by their £20,000 capital profit.

In some cases you may need to wait for the property to increase in value and give you the capital profit, so you need to make sure that you can fund the cash flow loss until you can take advantage of the capital profit.

Let's take a look at how this works practically when applying **My 2 Year Cash Flow Rule**.

I have kept the structure very simple: it's based on a freehold property without including a lot of the provisions and allowances. The actual **2 Year Cash Flow** worksheet that I use is available on my website at *www.3plus1plan.com*.

PART A – Acquisition Costs

NOTE	ACQUISITION COSTS SUMMARY			
A	Valuation		£100,000	
B	Valuation Free			£350
C	Amount of Mortgage	85%		£85,000
D	Deposit to Complete	15%		£15,000
E	Mortgage Broker Fees	0.50%		£400
F	Legal Costs			£1,000
G	Stamp Duty	0%		0
H	**Total Acquisition Cost of Purchase: £16,750**			

Initial acquisition costs in order to own the property on day one

A. **Valuation** – This is the RICS or Royal Institute of Chartered Surveyors valuation for mortgage purposes.

B. **Valuation fee** – This is the amount you will need to pay to the mortgage broker or lender to have the property valued. The result of the valuation is shown in A.

C. **Amount of the mortgage** – This is the amount of mortgage you have been offered, normally around 65%–85% for a buy to let property.

D. **Deposit required to complete** – Most cases you will require between 5% to 25% deposit to purchase the property.

E. **Mortgage broker fees** – These are the fees that the broker will charge you for arranging a mortgage. Normally between free and 1%.

F. **Legal costs** – This is to pay for the conveyance and any searches. Normally between £600 and £1,500.

G. **Stamp duty** – In this case no stamp duty is payable as the property is under the threshold.

H. **Total acquisition cost of purchase** – This is the total amount you would need to pay in order to complete the property and take ownership. This is where most people make the mistake of thinking this is all the property has cost – £16,750.

Additional acquisition costs

NOTE	ADDITIONAL ACQUISITION COSTS	
I	Curtains / White Goods / Flooring	£800
J	Void Period - 8 week allowance	£914
K	Furniture - (May not be required)	£2,000
L	**Additional Acquisition Costs: £3,714**	

I. **Curtains** – You will need to put these into your new property. If it is second–hand the property may already have them.

J. **Void period** – The national average void period is about 29 days, but I don't subscribe to that. I will always allow an eight–week period for the first two years of ownership when buying a new–build property. This is made up of a six–week period to *get it let* after completion and then a further two weeks at a later date. The extra two weeks actually gives me another six weeks be-cause the tenant has to give at least four weeks' notice. This is normally plenty of time to get the property re–let. Apart from this, I only ever allow two weeks per year void period on the condition that I stay on top of the lettings.

K. **Furniture** – In some city centre locations you may have to provide furniture. As always, do your due diligence and be flexible to change: the object is to get the property let quickly. Consider that an average furniture pack costs you £2,500 for a two–bedroom apartment.

L. **Additional acquisition costs** – This is the total in order to have your property ready to rent. So our total is around £4,000.

	MONTHLY COSTS TO HOLD THE PROPERTY		
			Average per month
M	Rental received		£500
N	Agents fees (incl VAT)	10%	£58
			Net Rent received: £442
O	Monthly Mortgage Payment	£85,000 @ 6%	£425
P	Service Charges / Maintenance	£600 per year	£50
Q	Gas / Electric Safety Certificate	£50 per year	£7
R	Total monthly shortfall:		£40
S	Total shortfall to be Quarantined: (R x 24 months = S):		£960
T	**Total amount required to buy and hold this property for a full 2 years (H + L + S = T):**		**£21,424**

M. **Rental received** – This is the realistic market rent you will receive, not the rent on the valuation for mortgages purposes.

N. **Agent's fees** – This is what the agent will charge you for finding a tenant and managing the property. The fees range from 8% up to 17% and don't forget to add in VAT.

O. **Monthly mortgage payment** – I only ever choose interest-only payments.

P. **Service charge/maintenance** – This could include a whole range of things from buildings insurance, payments to a sinking fund for future major repairs, general maintenance, security, cleaning and gardening – in fact, anything to do with the upkeep of the property. One of the benefits of a leasehold property is that this is organised for you and all you do is pay a single service charge.

Q. **Gas / Electric Safety Certificate** – You must undertake regular checks of any gas and electricity in your property.

R. Total monthly profit / shortfall – This is the amount of total profit / shortfall per month. As an average, in the UK it will range somewhere between £500 profit through to £500 shortfall per property.

S. Total profit / shortfall for two years – This is simply the total monthly profit / shortfall multiplied by 24 months.

T. Total required for 2 Year Cash Flow – This is the total amount you should set aside prior to completion of this property to enable you to **Set and Forget** it for a full two years.

Somewhere during the due diligence, the questions and the working-out of the figures, you will find exactly what your cash flow will be. If it shows a potential deficit, then you will work out how you are going to be able to guarantee payment of any deficits, and you set aside this deficit, normally in a provision account. As I say, 'fully funded for a full two years'.

That is the route to happy, successful property investing. Once you have realised the importance of your cash flow, you are on route to being a successful user of **The 3+1 Plan**.

Chapter 5

WHICH PORTFOLIO BUILDING STRATEGY WILL BE BEST FOR YOU?
STOP AT THREE PROPERTIES OR BUILD A LARGER PORTFOLIO?

I used to own a personal development company, listening to many different people left me with the realisation that most people are primarily motivated by two things: the desire *to increase pleasure and, the desire to avoid pain.*

Applied to **The 3+1 Plan**, avoiding pain is usually a financial concern, a fear that governments around the world are no longer going to provide a suitable retirement and that people are in real danger of being left short in later years. It's this fear that has motivated so many to turn to people like me, to help them avoid the pain of an unfunded retirement.

The desire to increase their pleasure is really a wish to enjoy life more, to enhance their lifestyle. The same desire is what drives me to invest in property, because **The 3+1 Plan** can achieve both objectives; removing the fear of an unfunded retirement while allowing you time to create a better lifestyle.

Lifestyle enhancement doesn't always mean buying big expensive toys. You will probably be surprised to find that what rates highest on many of my clients' lists is quite modest. Here are some of the most common reasons for building a portfolio:

- Dinners in fancy restaurants
- A weekly cleaner for the home
- Regular travel
- Staying in a luxury hotel rather than a budget hotel
- Business class and first class travel
- Babysitters on call
- Regular clothes shopping
- Catching a taxi rather than public transport
- A massage every week in their own home (ok, that one is mine)

You can probably think of many more. The important thing is that whilst people may be turned on by the big toys (houses, boats, cars), it's the little everyday conveniences that make the true difference and increase the quality of your life now. Often you don't require a massive portfolio to achieve these. It's one of the reasons why **The 3+1 Plan** works so well.

But now I'm going to suggest to you that there is a world beyond the 3+1 properties. Don't panic. You will build your portfolio only as large and as quickly as is right for you.

Originally I thought **The 3+1 Plan** would be the focus of most of the portfolios that I helped clients to build, but experience has now shown that very few people actually stopped at just 3+1.

Call it human greed or call it human nature, I think it is more that it is in our nature to want to provide for our loved ones and ourselves. So once they see that **The 3+1 Plan** works, then many people just want to go on.

Rather than go back to the drawing board I began to look at what it would take to achieve **The 3+1 Plan**, but without having to pay off your mortgages.

My FOUR portfolio building strategies

It didn't take long to work out that 7–10 properties with mortgages held for 7–10 years, would give a similar result to having 3+1 properties without mortgages.

So the **7–10 x 7–10 Strategy** was born. Buy 7–10 properties and hold them for 7–10 years.

I soon realised that this was a little bit scary to investors just starting out. The thought of 7–10 properties was too big a jump. So I thought about what was comfortable for a beginner and my

1, 2 STOP Strategy was born. It simply says: 'Buy a couple of properties and stop investing'.

Around the same time people began to ask why we stop at 7–10 properties and this seemed like a fair question. So I added **The Question Mark Strategy** and the question was: How many properties do you want, to fund the lifestyle you desire?

The last strategy to arrive was my **5 and Hold Strategy**. This was born out of experience. I took a number of clients from zero to 10 properties in under six months. Talk about an emotional roller coaster! I also began to realise that along the way, we had built the portfolio so fast that the basic systems for managing the portfolio were missing. So the **5 and Hold Strategy** was about holding off further investing until they were happy that their **Set and Forget** systems were working.

Let's look at each one in more detail.

1. 1, 2 STOP STRATEGY

Buy a couple of properties and stop investing

This strategy is simple: buy a couple of properties and STOP investing. By stopping there, you allow time to build your education level and also to develop your emotional intelligence. This is so fundamental. If you go out tomorrow and buy ten properties, emotionally you are going to be a nervous wreck, as you are stepping so far out of your comfort zone.

By saying 1, 2 STOP, you allow time for your comfort zone to expand at the rate of your education and experience. So it's an experiential learning approach, which is much better than any seminar or book. **You're learning a bit, doing a bit, learning a bit more, doing a bit more.**

This is the most fundamental of all the strategies. I designed it for beginner investors to use in the buy to let market.

One or two properties allow you to experience the practical side of the process: buying, finding tenants, dealing with agents, arranging mortgages and every other aspect of the property process.

Although the practical side is very important, I consider that the real power of the strategy lies in its ability to allow you to develop as an investor, mentally and emotionally, without overwhelming you with too much, too quickly. The reasoning is that by stopping after two, you allow your emotional state to catch up with your portfolio.

The only thing to consider now is how long to stop

This is totally dependent on you. Don't consider investing until you are 100% ready. By the same token, if you're a year down the track and haven't resumed, then you may well be resting in your comfort zone.

To put this strategy into perspective, let me tell you about John.

John paid his house off a long time ago and was earning an income of around £30,000 per year. He had already concluded that he could not afford to start building a significant property portfolio. Meanwhile, his home doubled in value once, twice, three times over the years, which left him with a considerable amount of equity that he wasn't making use of.

When he spoke to me for the first time, he mentioned that for years he knew that he had to do something, but in that time he had been fearful of using his equity. He worried about not being able to find tenants, crashing property prices, and all of the other beginner-investor issues.

These are fears spawned from a lack of investment education. In these cases, it's vital to try to replace outdated beliefs with a new set of enlightened ones. Once I explained everything, and went over the **1, 2 STOP Strategy** with him, he was ready to make his first purchase.

Check the Set and Forget Checklist

Once you have two properties then I recommend you run through Part A of **My Set and Forget Checklist**. This checklist will consider the basic systems that you should begin to consider as you build your portfolio to five properties. You can download a blank copy of the checklist on **The 3+1 Plan** website, www.3plus1plan.com. You don't need to wait until you have done the checklist in full. In fact, you can choose to leave a lot of it.

How do you get from 2 to 5 Properties?

It's really quite simple. Do the same things as you did to get the first two properties. This reminds me of a little saying I have always remembered on how to be successful:

Step 1. Learn how to do the right thing.
Step 2. Do the right thing.
Step 3. Repeat step 2 until it isn't the right thing anymore, then return to step 1.

It might sound simple but in essence that is exactly what I have done and so have millions of successful people before me. It doesn't matter what endeavour you are in. Learn how to do the right thing (whatever it is in your field, in this case property) and then simply do that thing over and over and over again. Don't change it until it no longer works for you.

So, if the first two properties worked for you, simply do the third, fourth and fifth in the same way.

Property is not rocket science

Property is not rocket science; you don't need 10 university degrees and years of study. You just need some good quality education (such as this book) and some real–life experience.

I tend to see an interesting thing happen as my clients begin to build their portfolio. At around five properties, an amazing realisation comes over them. They begin to realise that the same things happen on every property. They can even start to pre–empt what's going to happen. After all, they have experienced most of the variables before. After five properties, there really isn't much more they need to learn. The foundation is built, backed by good solid experience.

2. 5 AND HOLD STRATEGY

Build your portfolio to five properties and hold off investing further

For most people starting off as property investors, the thought of owning five properties is way out of any imaginable comfort zone. Most of us can imagine owning a couple of properties, but five properties present a whole range of new issues as you now have a certifiable property portfolio. So once you've completed **1,2 Stop** and built your portfolio to five properties, the next strategy is what I call my **5 and Hold Strategy.**

You simply need to build to five properties – then HOLD OFF investing further. The reason for this is that you need to make sure you have established the specific systems to run your portfolio easily – for example, setting up bank accounts correctly, setting up direct debits, filing all your paperwork, all the little systems that ensure that you can **Set and Forget** your portfolio.

In the process of getting to five properties, you will have set up some of these systems, you may have even completed Part A of **My Set and Forget Checklist**, but if you are like most investors, you would have been so preoccupied with learning about property that you will forget the little things.

That's why I suggest you hold at five properties and wait – for as long as you need, although I normally say six months minimum to really take things in and bed down a great foundation. Then, once all these things are in place and you are comfortable, you can continue. Crucially, it also gives you time to grow your emotional intelligence – to grow into a serious investor.

My **5 and Hold Strategy** is a recent addition to the four–stage process of building a portfolio from zero to ten properties. It arose from feedback I received from a number of my clients who built five properties very quickly. In most cases, they complained about the amount of paperwork that was piling up, constantly asking questions about things they should know but didn't because they weren't organised enough.

After having bought five properties and upgrading their lifestyle significantly and, spending money that should have been set aside for cash flow, Bill and Mary had not been paying their service charges or ground rents and had ignored just about every letter that they had received to do with property. Building their portfolio too quickly had taken its toll on them. They were in serious danger of losing it all unless they changed their ways.

Another client arrived at a portfolio review with two county court judgements because they had not paid their service charge notices.

You might think this is just plain stupid, but, let's face it, sometimes life can get in the way. For this very reason, it's important to get your systems set up right.

I have integrated each of my systems into a checklist, which we will cover in detail in this book. It will direct your attention and make it very easy to manage your growing portfolio. You don't need to follow this checklist to the letter to be successful; in fact, a lot of my clients have applied the same principles in different ways. Find what works for you and do it.

By the end of this stage you should truly be a professional investor with a thorough understanding of building a portfolio.

Remember, it's all about **Set and Forget**. The better you **Set** your portfolio up, the more you can **Forget** the portfolio on an ongoing basis.

Bringing the future results into present view

The second aspect of **5 and Hold** is setting and beginning to incorporate some *lifestyle* goals. This is where you need to sit down and decide some very specific goals to achieve the lifestyle you want. At the end of the day, that's why we're building a portfolio – *lifestyle.*

That's why I am so passionate about goals and lifestyle as an integral part of building a thriving property portfolio. Remember: building a portfolio should give you more life.

I tend to find that until you have five properties, you have very little idea about just how much is really possible through property. Your **3+1 Plan** will give you the pension you wanted, but achieving your fifth property tends to open your eyes to the lifestyle possibilities. It's also about the time when you stop talking in terms of *how many* properties you own and start talking about *how much* they are worth.

'How much' is more important than 'How many'

When we first start investing in property we start off with a goal of one or two properties; rarely do we actually think about how much the property is worth or even refer to our portfolio as a figure. It's always one property, two properties, three properties. In my experience, at around five properties a transformation takes place. You begin to recognise that the value of the portfolio is what's important, not the number of properties.

The one property, two properties, three properties becomes £1 million pounds, £2 million pounds. This is an important transformation.

3. MY 7–10 X 7–10 STRATEGY

Buy 7–10 properties and hold them for 7–10 years

Welcome to the practical development of **The 3+1 Plan**. In truth, **3+1** with no mortgages is a great theoretical premise, but you can achieve a better and quicker outcome with 7–10 properties, *all with mortgages.*

My **7–10 x 7–10 Strategy** is simply that you should buy 7–10 properties, and hold them for 7–10 years. This strategy works on one assumption: that property will double every 7–10 years. It has followed this pattern over the past fifty odd years and there is no reason why it won't continue to do so, because it is based on one very important thing.

The law of supply and demand

The law of supply and demand is that part of economics which focuses on the allocation of scare resources and the changing value of such resources. It essentially means that scarce things are more valuable than abundant things (that's the supply side) and things that people want are more valuable than things that people don't want (that's the demand side).

Of course, supply and demand is based on one thing that hasn't changed much in thousands of years: human nature. Human nature is simply the tendency of humans to act in a predicable way, based on their genetics, social programming and personal experience. **It's because of this that I believe so strongly that property prices, rents and the costs involved in property will continue to spiral upwards.**

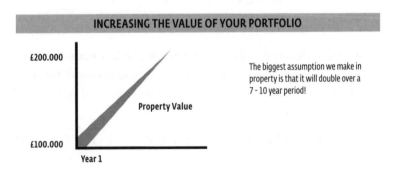

INCREASING THE VALUE OF YOUR PORTFOLIO

£200.000

Property Value

£100.000

Year 1

The biggest assumption we make in property is that it will double over a 7 - 10 year period!

So, buy 7–10 properties and hold them for 7–10 years. The property is going to double in value, which will create a significant amount of equity; this will then self–fund your retirement. At the end of the day, that's what it's all about –reaching a position where your retirement is fully looked after. Along the way, you're going to set some goals and reach them– that is what really excites me about property.

Why do I think 7–10 properties doubling over 7–10 years will be able to fund your retirement and provide for your future better? The value of your portfolio will have doubled, your rents will have doubled and your costs will have remained low, because you have only paid the interest on your mortgages.

The proper question then is 'When should I pay off my mortgages?' First, when should I pay off my home mortgage? Second, 'When should I pay off my buy to let properties?'

a. Let's deal with the home first

Yes, you should pay off your home eventually, because it is a non–tax–deductible expense if it relates to your principle place of residence. Okay, that was the accountant in me speaking and, since I leave the accounting to my accountant, let me put my investor hat back on.

The extension of that answer is that until you have built up a portfolio adequate to maintain momentum, in most cases you will have no choice but to leverage your home. I think it is safe to say that most people have a home with significant equity and this equity is the key to building wealth.

By accessing this equity and using the leverage of a mortgage

on the buy to let properties, you can turn £100,000 equity into a million pound portfolio.

The sole purpose for this is to gain the advantage of capital growth. Until such time as your portfolio sustains its own growth you cannot afford to pay off your mortgage.

Once you have developed your portfolio, then and only then, can you take your principle place of residence out of the investment portfolio.

I remember a chat with Phil and Alison who were reluctant to use the equity in their home to begin funding the growth of their portfolio. They had trouble with the emotional challenge of mortgaging something that they had been told their whole lives they should pay off.

I told them to think of it this way: rather than borrowing from the home and never paying it back, I told them to see it as taking a five-year loan from their home. They would have every intention of paying it back in full in five years time. This gave them five years to build their property portfolio and have it return enough to pay back the loan on the home.

b. Now for the investment properties

When you consider that the biggest challenge to building a portfolio is maintaining cash flow, why would you pay additional money into the property, when you know that it's going to double in the next 7–10 years?

You should never pay your mortgage down on these, and you should always opt for interest only. That way your mortgage

balance will stay the same throughout, but your value will double, effectively cutting your mortgage in half or more.

You are far better reinvesting the cash flow in more property. In the long–term, this is a more effective use of your capital and cash flow and it limits the amount of tax you will pay.

But as always it depends on the outcome you are looking to achieve.

4. THE QUESTION MARK STRATEGY

How many properties do you need to fund the lifestyle you desire? That's a personal question and until you get to the position of having built a significant portfolio, you can't begin to understand how much lifestyle you will create through property. Through remortgaging, selling and cash flow, the lifestyle you can create is fantastic.

So, how are you going to become rich? This is a one of those questions that most people ask at some point, especially as they build their portfolio and are waiting for the market to turn.

First, let me qualify the word 'rich'.

I don't help people to become rich. I don't create millionaires. I help people move to a position of financial freedom. Here's an example of how that might work. Let's say you purchase three flats, all worth £100,000 and they require £100 per month or £1,200 per year. So you need to subsidise the portfolio by £3,600 per year, assuming that rents and mortgage payments all stay the same over the period.

The biggest assumption that we make in property, as I keep repeating, is that it will double every 7–10 years. So let's assume that it takes ten years this time. That means that you have funded the properties to the tune of £36,000 over the ten years. The properties should have gone up by £300,000 (3 properties x £100,000) making you a profit of £264,000 pounds. Right?

Well, not exactly, and this is where most people initially lose their way. Yes, you have made that money (let's forget taxes and interest rate variations right now and focus on strategy), but it is highly unlikely that you are going to sit on the three properties for ten years. This is where the real power of leverage and compounding in your portfolio takes effect.

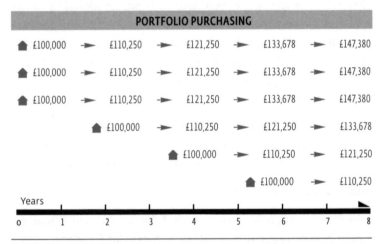

Once we have spent our initial capital we use the capital created within the portfolio to secure our retirement

Assume that you keep the properties for two years and funded the £7,200 (2 years x £3600) required to hold the properties. You have properties worth £300,000. Let's say that over this period they go up by only 5% per year. So they are worth £315,000 at the end of the first year and £330,750 by the end of the second year.

Assuming you remortgage now, you could take up to £281,137 (£330,750 x 85%) minus the previous mortgage £255,000 (£300,000 x 85%). So you are left with a net total of £26,137. Then you need to take away the £7,200 you have invested so far and I also suggest you take the £7,200 for the next two years. This leaves you with £11,737.

Now this is decision time – do you take the money and run? Or do you reinvest the money in another property?

If you *spend it,* then you may have another two years to wait until you can potentially remortgage again.

If you *reinvest it,* you have another property worth £100,000 and your portfolio is worth £430,000. Assuming it goes up 5% again for the first two years, you will then have a portfolio worth £474,000 and a mortgage of £366,137.

So let's remortgage at 85% again and you can take out £402,900, leaving you £36,763 minus the £2,400 you need to hold the property (remember you allowed the cash flow for the other three already, so you only need to allow for the extra property) and the £9,600 for the following two years (4 properties x 2 years x £100 per month). This leaves you around £25,000.

Again, your decision is whether to spend it or invest it. Let's say you decide to do a bit of both. You spend £10,000, reinvest £10,000 and the other £5,000 you just put aside for a rainy day.

So you purchase another £100,000 property and the cycle repeats and repeats and repeats. Over time you begin to take more and more money out in the form of remortgages (and occasionally selling). You could even allow the mortgages to stick where they are and allow the rent to increase to create some increased cash flow for you.

A couple of important things to consider:

- As you invest in more property, you will have larger sums of cash available. This can be used to fund the cash flow on the property (during the stagnant times) or it can be used to fund your growing lifestyle.
- I am a big believer in never, ever selling, so after ten years you ideally renew the property or, if you must, sell it and then replace it with a new property. The strategy of never selling means that the capital gains will never become an issue for you.

So let me finally answer the question about being rich. The true question is how many properties do you require and how much does your portfolio need to be worth in order to fund your lifestyle? Only you can answer that.

Chapter 6

THE CRYSTAL BALL OF PROPERTY
ALWAYS REMEMBER THE HISTORIC PROPERTY CYCLES

It never ceases to amaze me how many people go into property for the long term, yet they really expect to consistently pull large amounts of money out after one or two years.

Most of the time this just isn't going to happen. **Investing in property is a 7–10 year event and, if you treat it with respect, it will pay huge dividends.**

I tell all my clients that the sooner you change your real expectations for property – from some *get rich quick, fly by night expedition into a long-term emotional change and lifestyle journey* – the sooner you can sit back and enjoy the experiences, relationships and lifestyle choices it allows.

The wonderful thing about property is that it has followed very clear cycles over the past sixty (and arguably more) years. In fact, in the past fifteen years it has become even more stable and predictable, which is great news for all property investors.

Even the most recent downturn in 2008/2009 was a predictable part of a normal boom / bust cycle, no matter how many news stories say this time it was different.

The property cycle over the past fifty years has doubled approximately every 7.3 years. Of those years, it will normally decrease or stagnate for one to two years, grow at between 2% to 5% for three to eight years and best of all grow between 10% to 25% for between two to three years.

These property cycles allow educated property investors to crystal ball gaze and, with some degree of accuracy, predict what the cycle will be doing for the next couple of years (or at least with enough accuracy to make money!)

The simple way of explaining a quite intricate set of dynamics *is that it shoots up, stagnates and then shoots up again.*

There are four phases:

1. Steady / watch cash flow
2. Stagnate / buy
3. Galloping / buy / remortgage
4. Galloping / restructuring

Before I jump into explaining each of the phases, you need to understand that these phases will give you an idea into the general trends of property in each phase. You may find that an individual property 'bucks the trend'. As a property professional I use trends to predict the most appropriate strategy for the phase and I use an understanding of good solid fundamentals to know the merits of each individual property.

PHASE 1: STEADY / WATCH CASH FLOW

The 'Steady / Watch Cash Flow' phase is the 'boring' phase of the property cycle.

I use the word 'steady', because throughout this phase, your property may not really do much at all. It is likely to remain at the same value or in some areas it may increase slightly, while others may decrease. The important understanding here is that, unless you are selling, you will not notice much difference.

I use the phrase 'Watch Cash Flow', because during this period, the interest rates are likely to increase early in the cycle and remain high throughout it. So the emphasis is on watching your cash flow. **Throughout this phase, cash flow is your primary consideration.**

Your property is unlikely to sell easily, because of sluggish demand. Attempting to refinance could present a problem, because of high interest rates. Property sales during this phase will likely be very slow, and asking prices are definitely negotiable. The start of this phase is what we call a buyer's market.

It's a buyer's market because we have just come out of a period of massive price growth, and most people have made significant money in the market. The interest rates have started to increase, causing turbulence in the market and many investors want to take their profits and run.

The newspapers will be predicting a price crash (or, as they call it, the 'bubble bursting') and some investors will want to take their profits and offload their property.

This is your opportunity.

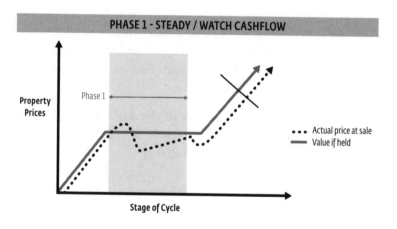

I remember Peter saying that you can make the most money in property when prices are going down. He went on to say that this was not because the prices were actually going down, but because everyone was talking about them going down. My experience has been the same.

The essential tactic in the start of this phase is the ridiculous offer.

Choose a property you want and decide how much you are willing to pay for it. And then drop it by 10%, 20% or even 30%. The actual offer will depend how bad people fear things are and how bad they fear they might get. This will give you your starting bid. Be prepared for some rejection, but even if only one in 20 ridiculous offers are accepted, you've snapped up quite a bargain!

The basic strategy in this phase is holding: only buy when you are sure you can 'cash flow' for the long term.

Phase 2: Stagnate / Buy

This phase of the property cycle sees an easing of previous cash flow and a stagnation or possible downturn in capital growth. The strategy for this phase is preparation and relief. You've survived the hard times in terms of cash flow and you're on your way back to the good times.

Now, make no mistake: **the order of the day for this phase is uncertainty and fear.** The papers will be talking everything down. You have to see through all of this.

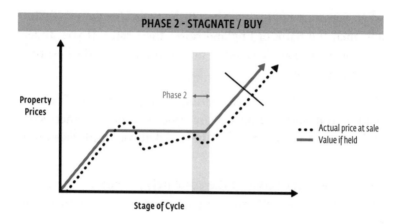

I use the word 'stagnate', because the economic cycle is such that you will see a slowing of economic growth (often on a worldwide scale). Interest rates may begin to drop and this will counteract the effect of slowing economic growth, and after a time it will create a more buoyant market.

You'll notice that each time the rate comes down your cash flow eases. Enjoy this extra cash flow for a while, but it's important not to go crazy and buy too much, too early. Interest rates can still go up.

The major consideration here is that property prices will come under downward pressure because of lagging demand. There will be a lot of talk of recession and prices dropping. At the end of Phase 1, it's normal for the papers to say that 30% drops are possible and that the price–to–earnings ratio is unsustainable.

This phase can seem to go on forever before the market really heats up, but the danger in this phase is that the Bank of England lowers rates and sits on that rate for six months or more. The worst thing you can do here is to jump the gate too early. This is when you start buying with too little regard for your cash flow and then the Bank of England raises their rates. If you understand why rates are lowered or raised, you'll know the best time to jump in again.

Nor do you really want to be selling during this phase, if you can hold onto it until the next phase. Sales will be extremely slow, and expect to accept offers well below what you think your property is worth.

Again, this is the phase of the absolutely ridiculous offer. Buying in this phase will astound you. Your ridiculous offers will be accepted.

PHASE 3: GALLOPING / BUY / REMORTGAGE

This is where property gets a lot more exciting! This stage will start with talk of recession: ignore it and concentrate on the asset prices.

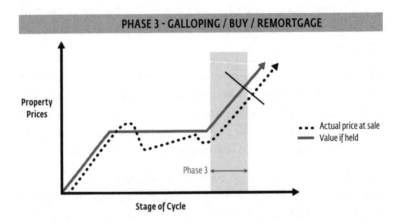

I use the word 'galloping', because interest rates will be low, properties everywhere will be increasing in value and, as time goes on, the market will get hotter and hotter. Eventually the whole market will seem unstoppable (and probably is, for a time at least).

It's like a horse galloping along, majestic and unstoppable. This is the time when you can make an offer on a property and, before you can exchange, you are 'gazumped' by a higher–priced bidder.

It's an unfortunate fact of buying property in Britain and Wales that up until exchange the seller can decline your offer, at any point and with no reason whatsoever. Normally, this would be because they have received a better offer, but it could come down to them just deciding not to sell anymore.

This will mean that any costs incurred so far in valuations, surveys and conveyance, will be yours to bear. Buying new build will normally mean that gazumping will be limited, but it is always a possibility.

During this phase your strategy should simply be to buy and refinance. And then buy some more.

Prices will never be this low again. You can buy freely in this stage. The ridiculous offer is out the door, and don't be surprised if you have to pay full price and perhaps even more, as prices are negotiated upward.

Cash flow is normally not the issue during this phase, the amount of capital available is.

During this period, when selling property is easy, it is often harder to achieve big discounts, as builders and owners do not have to worry about sales. This is why you often require more capital. The only caution is not to ride the wave too long. You'll have certain indicators of when to slow down and begin restructuring and that's the point when you'll need to move onto the next phase.

PHASE 4: GALLOPING / RESTRUCTURING

The market will still be galloping along and you will have made a nice little profit from it. Sitting on your hands and not buying another 'deal' is by far the hardest thing to do in property. But sit you must. **Stop buying and start creating an equity buffer.**

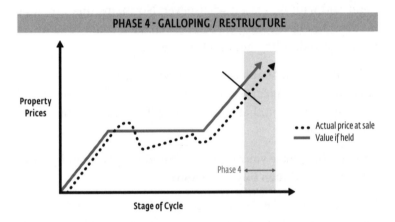

At some point in the future the market is going to slow down and even recess, so you must restructure your portfolio, as cash flow is the primary consideration again. There will be telltale signs of the change coming. The Bank of England will be talking about having to get inflation in check; the newspapers will be predicting the bubble bursting.

As we approach the Stagnant Phase your property's growth will begin to slow as interest rates rise. Your cash flow will become tighter and you will need to use your equity buffer to fund this in the future.

You achieve this in one or both of the following ways:

How much you need to restructure will depend on your portfolio, but you may need to sell some of your properties and place the proceeds straight into your mortgages to correct any cash flow deficiencies.

The second way involves remortgaging your properties to their maximum, using a flexible or offset facility, which simply means that you have a maximum limit you can draw upon, but you only pay interest on the amount you owe at the time.

You will use this cash flow to fund any shortfalls through the long steady and stagnant periods of Phase 1 and Phase 2. Never forget, though, that you never know how long each phase will last.

Lack of cash flow will cause your property to be repossessed, but a lack of capital or negative equity will simply stop you from buying more.

We've jumped ahead a little because the key to this part of the cycle is picking the right time to stop and restructure: too early and you're not maximising your returns; too late and you could be in for a serious reality check. Picking the right time is perhaps the hardest aspect of **The 3+1 Plan**.

I once had a conversation with Jonas, who started with four properties that he bought through stagnant and stable phases. The galloping market came, and he began a purchasing frenzy. Still, no complaints! Throughout the galloping phase, he maintained the same frantic pace of remortgaging for equity and then using that equity to buy more.

By the end of the galloping phase he had 30 properties in his port-folio. 'Fantastic!' you say? Well, I wasn't quite so comfortable and had a sense of what would most likely come next. Sure enough, he'd kept on buying right through Phase 4 – galloping / restructur-ing – and ended up with forty–nine properties! Talk about throw-ing caution to the wind!

So, as you might expect, as interest rates rose, so did his monthly repayments. He tried putting his properties on the market, but they were all mortgaged to the hilt and even if he did sell, they had grown so quickly that the capital gains liability would have removed any chance of a profit.

One year on, he was back down to twelve properties (the rest be-ing in the process of being repossessed and all being sold at abso-lute bargain prices) and he had well and truly ruined his credit rating. So purchasing property is not an option for him in the foreseeable future.

I asked him what he thought would have happened if he'd stopped buying at fifteen or twenty properties and, instead, started re-structuring his portfolio.

As we played with numbers it became clear that had he stopped and done nothing but remortgage at 20, the equity he would have had would have seen him through the stagnant phase.

So what's the lesson here for you? It's simply this. Beware the ego trip.

One of the biggest obstacles that new investors face after they begin to see success is the ego trip.

It normally takes place when the market is rising quickly and capital appreciation is huge. These investors begin to see some real money coming in through remortgages, property sales and cash flow from low interest rates.

Most of the time they begin to get a sense of invincibility, a feeling they can buy anything and make money; they begin to disregard the very principles that got them there in the first place. Let's face it, the property shows on television make it all look so easy.

It is very easy to think that the galloping market will continue forever. It won't.

Often, investors will realise the mistake of over–committing their capital when interest rates begin to rise after the boom. Their cash flow will struggle and they will find it difficult to sell the properties they were relying on selling.

I am a big believer in 'Slow and steady wins the race.'

So many times, I have seen people build a portfolio, only to have to sell it up when they have realised they didn't cash flow it. They bought over–price, they didn't conduct proper due diligence, they believed a salesperson, or they just got plain lazy.

Stick to the principles in this book and you will consistently pass the sleep test and be able to **Set and Forget** your portfolio, knowing that success in **The 3+1 Plan** will be just around the corner.

Chapter 7

MAKE MORE MONEY BY MAKING YOUR PORTFOLIO GROW FASTER
THREE STRATEGIES TO ENHANCE YOUR LIFE AND YOUR PROFITS

The goal of investing in property is to make money, lots of money, to ease the stress of day–to–day life. The essence of achieving this is actually very simple, and it just needs you to follow some or all of these straightforward strategies.

- **Buy property and flip it**
- **Buy, complete and sell**
- **Buy, complete, let and hold**

Let's take a look in detail at each of these points. I've split them under two categories: New build / Off–plan; and Second–hand property.

New Build / Off–plan Strategies

New build / Off–plan property presents a host of advantages over second–hand property. Three basic strategies can help you maximise the value of your property portfolio and a mixture of all three is essential to maintain your portfolio's growth.

Strategy 1: Buy and flip prior to completion

If there is a long build time, then the value of your off plan property can appreciate significantly before it even completes. At any time after exchange, you can choose to flip or reassign the contract to another party and take the capital growth as profit. Here's an example of that strategy in action:

You exchange contracts on a property for £100,000 with a £5,000 deposit paid immediately. You then become the owner of the equitable interest in the property, which means that you own any capital growth that the property experiences from that point on.

After 12 months, the property has appreciated in value to £120,000, so you decide to flip it. Through a local estate agent you locate a buyer who will pay £120,000. In order to assign the contract the buyer pays to you the appreciated value of the property (£20,000) plus your deposit (£5,000). You're now free to move to your next property!

Obviously, it is important to time your flip well. If you flip too early, you could limit your potential growth; if you flip too late you might not be able to sell it and therefore have to complete yourself.

Strategy 2: Buy, complete and sell

With this strategy, you hold onto the property until it's built. Once finished, you place the property on the market at the appreciated value and take the profit. Here's a quick example:

You purchase the property for £100,000, with £5,000 deposit paid when the contract is exchanged, and £10,000 deposit paid on completion. At completion, the property has appreciated and is valued at £130,000. You put it on the market for £130,000 and sell it. You receive £45,000 when you sell (£15,000 deposit back plus £30,000 in appreciation value).

The benefit of this strategy over the first is that the property is completed, so your buyer can mortgage the property, allowing you to receive the full appreciated value. It is also easier to sell a property that is built, since buyers love the thought of actual bricks and mortar.

This is an excellent strategy if the property is not suited to buy to let, if you require the capital to continue to build your portfolio, or you may have problems letting the property.

Remember with both strategies 1 & 2 you will no longer own the property; this goes against the ultimate goal of building a portfolio. So be warned, you should only flip or sell if you cannot justify the returns you will receive through keeping the property.

STRATEGY 3: BUY, COMPLETE, LET AND HOLD

This is certainly the best strategy if cash flow is not a problem, as you are building a portfolio rather than just creating capital.

It brings into play the landlord duties of finding and letting to tenants, but I always recommend that you find a full management letting agent who handles everything for you. The beauty of this strategy is that you benefit from all of the capital appreciation and cash flow.

*It is vital that you realise that you are an investor not a landlord. As I have repeatedly stressed, my underlying philosophy is **Set and Forget** property. This means that you should not have to manage and maintain your investments along the way, but instead, leave that with experienced professionals while you sit back and enjoy the benefits to your lifestyle.*

Astute buyers can utilise the above three strategies across multiple developments or even in a single property, as long as they understand the constraints of cash flow and the potential risks.

What I mean by this is that you can reserve and exchange two or even three properties, knowing full well that you do not wish to complete on all the transactions. You can do this in anticipation that the capital appreciation will be sufficient to 'flip' one or two, and use the monies from this to fund the completion of the others.

This obviously increases the risk, but with experience you will be able to combine these strategies very safely and in some cases you may choose not to flip properties at all.

Let's look at one of my clients in this scenario:

John had reserved three properties in a development, all valued at £135,000. He paid an initial deposit of 5% or £20,250. Upon completion he was to pay a further 5% and use a gifted deposit for the other 5% to make up the 15% deposit. While John had enough money to cover all the deposits and costs to complete, his aim was to 'flip' one or two of the properties prior to completion. This way he could effectively get the third property for free.

About six months prior to completion he put the three properties on the market for £170,000 each. After two months of marketing he accepted an offer on one of the flats at £160,000. After exchanging he received the 5% deposit back (£8,000) from the flat. Once the flat he sold completed, he received the difference between £160,000 and £135,000 or £25,000. He completed as normal on the other two flats.

All in all he required £27,000 plus costs to complete on the two flats, but received back from the sale £25,000. So his input into the deal was only £2,000 plus costs for two flats. Not a bad outcome.

John's biggest risk here was not being able to sell the property at a profit. Should he be unable to sell the property he would be required to come up with the completion monies for all three properties.

WHICH IS BETTER: NEW BUILD OR OFF PLAN PROPERTY?

In order to decide on the most appropriate strategy you need to understand the relative pros and cons of new build and off plan property.

New build (or 'stock') is classified as a development that is within three months of completion, or has completed, but has not yet been tenanted.

Off plan is a development that is longer than three months from completion or even where the property has not moved earth yet.

Some people may say that off plan is simply property that has not begun being built and technically they are correct. But let me explain why I consider it very different.

It's all about structure.

My definition is not really based on time, it is based more on the fact that in most cases, with newly built property you can exchange and complete at the same time or within a short time. This simply means that if you have structured correctly, your money will go into the property and come out very quickly, effectively realising your gain at purchase and exponentially growing your return on investment.

An off plan scenario is quite different. You would normally be expected to place a 5% – 10% deposit on exchange and then wait for completion, which could be up to a couple of years later. Only at this time could you realise a gain from the property: prior to this it is simply a paper gain.

Working out which one presents a better return depends on the market. You need to look at what the market is doing. This, in property, is what is called 'making your strategy meet the market'.

Let's consider two very different property markets, two different types of property and the relative results they achieve.

The stagnant market

If you purchase an **off plan** property that is due for completion in 18 months' time and place a 10% deposit down at exchange, then you would expect that because the market is stagnant, the property would not increase that much in value over that period.

Therefore you have paid 10% and made effectively no return, as the property has not really increased in price over this period. You also have the risk of the market changing, rents falling, prices falling, mortgage products changing and interest rates increasing. So you may find it difficult to secure a mortgage.

The problem here is that the market when you make your purchase decision is not necessarily the same market you will complete in. Herein lies your risk.

On the other hand if you purchased a **new build** property, you would have paid your deposit and, depending on your structure, received any discounts. The benefit of new build in a stagnant market is that the market that you are purchasing in is also the market that you will complete in. Quite simply, it's a lot safer.

Your actual cash tied up will be significantly less than the off plan scenario. This extra cash can then be used to purchase another property or cash flow an existing one.

Therefore, if you purchase off plan in a stagnant market, you are likely to buy one property as opposed to new build where, for the same cash input, you could buy perhaps three times as much property.

In a stagnant market, new build is a better proposition than off plan property.

The galloping market

The same two properties purchased in a galloping market would mean that the **new build** is still a decent proposition, except that you have to remember that you have a mortgage to service. It will certainly go up in value more than in a stagnant market, and, because interest rates may be low, your cash flow is eased.

Now consider the **off plan.** You still secure the property with a 10% deposit, but over the course of the build programme your property may have increased in value by 10%. You don't have a mortgage or cash flows to worry about.

Here is the power of off plan in a galloping market. Say the property is worth £200,000. You place a £20,000 deposit on it. If it goes up 10%, it goes up on the entire value (£200,000), not just your deposit. So you have just doubled your money before you have even completed – £200,000 x 10% = £20,000 or 100% return on investment albeit a paper profit before taxes, etc.

There is no doubt that in the galloping market the off plan can be a fantastic proposition. But don't get caught up in the hype of the sales pitch, thinking that doubling your money before completion is easy or automatic.

STRATEGIES FOR SECOND HAND PROPERTY

There are three main strategies in second hand property.

- Buy, hold and let
- Buy, renovate and sell
- Buy, renovate, let and hold

One of the greatest restrictions with second hand property is that, in most cases, you must take ownership of the property before you can benefit from the strategy you have applied. This ties up valuable capital and restricts the number of transactions you can undertake. It can also add to costs and may even present a potential holding problem with the property.

There is also a plus, in that with second hand property, because you own it and it's not new, you have the potential of adding real value by renovating the property. Done properly you can achieve this very quickly and then either hold onto it or sell it.

The most important strategy to be aware of at all time is never to buy above or even at the true value of a property. Astute property investors understand that the best profit is made when you purchase.

Everyone knows not to pay 'over the odds' for property, but few people realise that it is equally a sin to pay 'market value' or what the property is actually worth. Of course, the plan is to hold it as the value rises over time, but this can only be done by purchasing below a property's true valuation.

Whatever you do, do not listen to estate agents who tell you to 'buy now and wait for it to go up,' that 'it's a hotspot,' or that it has 'huge potential'. Make sure you have an **independent valuation** performed by a reputable company and then negotiate a discount off this value.

If you cannot get a discount, then do not buy. This may seem rather harsh but it is one of the fundamentals of property investment, and I cannot stress this enough.

Chapter 8

DO YOU WANT HELP IN HANDLING YOUR PORTFOLIO?

USING A PROPERTY CLUB CAN SAVE YOU MONEY, AND MORE IMPORTANTLY, YOUR TIME

Since the beginning of 2000 a new type of industry has emerged in the UK called the property investment company or Property Club. It's unlike an estate agency, in that it represents the buyers' interests rather than the sellers'.

Originally, many of these types of organisations were very sales focused. Some concentrated on buying and renovating, others on second hand property or land acquisitions and rezoning, but most stayed in the off plan and new build marketplace.

I first started in the property club industry in 1994 in Australia, and, when I moved to the UK, I began running the typical 'millionaire in two–to–five years' seminars that you so often see in the newspapers. But I soon realised that these seminars were selling pipe dreams, and what people really needed was help in making their dreams come true.

So, in 2004, I set up my company *YourPropertyClub.com,* which was originally focused on educating consumers about property investment principles. In fact, the source of much of this book comes from the 400 various articles that I originally wrote for clients.

Property clubs offer many benefits, especially for busy people who don't have the time to build a portfolio, but exactly what?

Anyone with a little knowledge of property investment can create their own portfolio. But I believe there are seven main reasons why anyone might welcome the help of a property investment organisation.

The benefits are these:

1. **Wide access to property**
2. **Experienced structuring of a deal**
3. **Reduced prices from bulk purchasing**
4. **Management of the buying process**
5. **Management of your portfolio**
6. **Regular reviews of your portfolio**
7. **The fees are less than you save**

1. WIDE ACCESS TO PROPERTY

The great thing about most property clubs is that they can source property throughout the UK. I have done deals as far north as Scotland and as far south as Southampton, from Grimsby across to Liverpool and over a hundred places in between. Working alone, there is no way you could cover this much distance.

I have a full-time team of three who do nothing other than source deals for me and they have around forty developers, as well as another five full-time sourcing people that they work with. This network of relationships allows my company to source much more property than we could ever need; this in turn allows us to be choosy about what property we take on.

2. STRUCTURING THE DEAL

One of the great things about using a property investment company is its ability to use various structures to ensure you use the minimal amount of capital. When you begin investing, you will probably use the simplest of structures to purchase property, which normally involves a 15% deposit, plus all the costs in the case of a buy to let property.

A property investment company will be able to guide you through the most effective use of your capital and should be able to cut down both your outlay and your time.

3. Save from bulk purchasing power

One of the best financial traits of an investment company is their ability to negotiate discounts on bulk purchases. Much the same as going to a supermarket, you get a special discount when you buy bulk. It's exactly the same principle in property.

These companies can negotiate large discounts over and above what individuals can achieve. If you walk in off the street, I always assume that you can negotiate at least a 5% discount off any individual property, but a company can negotiate a 12% discount off the asking price of a property because they have reserved 10 units. In some cases discounts can be between 5% and 35%, depending on the market.

Let's say in this example that the properties are worth £100,000 each and the company buys them for £88,000. The real financial advantage to you of using the company in this case is actually 7% or £7,000 (12% less 5% leaving 7%).

It's important to remember that if you are buying through a property investment company, you will still have all the normal costs associated with the purchase.

4. Management of the buying process

Today's busy society has left us with little time to do the things we need to do, let alone have the time to manage the process of buying property and building a portfolio. For this reason, above all others, a property investment company can be your best friend.

Most if not all companies will refer you to a broker, who will get the mortgage completed with the minimum of fuss. They will also refer you to a solicitor who can handle the conveyance issues involved. Some even help you get you your first tenant, furnish the place and organise the flooring and curtains.

5. Ongoing management of your portfolio

Portfolio management is what I see as the most important part of building a portfolio; it is also the least understood in the UK. This entire book is about building and growing your portfolio, but the ongoing management of the portfolio is the key. So many times we get so excited about buying the property that we neglect the ongoing holding of the property, and that's where the money is made.

A full portfolio management service will give you all the education you need, as long as you need it, rather than an all–in–one hit (as with a seminar).

This was perhaps the most important thing I learned as I got started in property. It's vital to have someone who is independent of your portfolio, a mentor, someone who can give you an unemotional, unattached view of your portfolio.

I have been lucky in my life: I have consistently found a number of people who were more than happy to provide me with clear direction and an insight into the next step. I was able to heed their counsel and grow my understanding and wealth. I am pig-headed at the best of times and a lot of the time, when they gave advice, I didn't fully understand it and therefore didn't apply it. I soon learned the lesson the hard way.

I have a story that has stuck with me for many years.

You are enrolled in a full-time informal course called 'life' and each day at this school you will have the opportunity to learn lessons. You may like the lessons or think them irrelevant or stupid. But lessons you will have.

There are no mistakes in life, only lessons. Your growth is a process of trial and error, of experiment, and the failed experiments are as much a part of the process as the experiment that ultimately works.

A lesson will be presented to you in various forms until you have learned to cope with it. Then you can go on to the next lesson.

There is no part of life that does not contain lessons; if you are alive, then you are still learning lessons.

This has stayed with me for a long time and I consistently remember its powerful message. Another way I like to explain its message is this.

You have lessons to learn from life. First, life will whisper softly in your ear. If you don't listen, it will tap you gently on the shoulder. If you don't listen, it will shake both your shoulders. If you still don't listen, it will take a block of four by two wood and smack you across the back of the head.

6. REGULAR REVIEWS OF YOUR PORTFOLIO

One of the key elements of **The 3+1 Plan** is regular reviews of what you have achieved and how to take the portfolio further. At the very heart of my strategies is the fact that you will need to remortgage the property on a regular basis in order to cash flow the portfolio for further periods. The decisions to do this will be based on decisions made during a review.

I strongly suggest that if you haven't found a mentor to help you build your portfolio, you start by using one of my portfolio managers to help you on your way. They will use the review checklist detailed below. It's essential that you get some professional support on a regular basis.

The topics that you will cover during each review will be:

	PORTFOLIO REVIEW CHECKLIST
1	How much capital you have available to fund your portfolio or purchase more property.
2	How much cash flow you require to fund each property into the future.
3	Amount of funds in the provision account, and the amount of funds required for the provision account.
4	The current value of each of your properties.
5	Which Properties can be remortgaged, and how much you can take out.
6	Whether the rental should be raised on any of your properties.
7	Review all of your mortgage products and whether you should change any.
8	Whether you require any major capital payments for lifestyle.
9	What the portfolio goals are from here.
10	Whether you are achieving the goals previously set out for the portfolio.
11	What areas of education you require to jump to the next level of understanding.
12	Whether you need to change any of the systems that enable you to Set and Forget your portfolio.

7. The fees are less than you save

So, what's the cost of using a property investment company? Most will charge a fee for the sourcing of each property between 2% and 4%. Most companies will leave it there, but others may charge for any number of additional things. Here's a list of other potential charges:

- Monthly fees between £20 and £120
- Joining fees between £500 and £5,000
- Weekend seminar fee between £395 and £5,995
- Aftercare services such as sourcing furniture, blinds, flooring (often at a premium)

You can see these costs can add up.

My company charges a flat fee every time you buy a property – I don't believe in all the other fees that some companies charge. They are extortionate for what you get in return.

Should you buy from a property investment company?

Personally, I've only ever bought through this type of company. For me, it's been worth it as everything was done for me and I've experienced total peace of mind. Well worth the money.

In contrast, I remember back to my first few properties in Australia and the trials and tribulations making money on them. I was buying and renovating them myself and it took so much of my time.

Sure I made money, but really, when you take into account the actual time and emotions that I spent while attending to my properties, I sometimes wonder if it was worth all the fuss.

A property investment company can be a fantastic way of getting into property easily and building a substantial portfolio with minimal capital. In fact, it can be pain–free and a downright delight. But as with anything in life, go in with your eyes wide open, trust no one, ask lots of probing questions, speak with existing customers and you should come out on top.

Chapter 9

DEVELOPING YOUR PORTFOLIO
YOUR PROPERTY WILL DO MORE THAN BEAT INFLATION; IT WILL CHANGE YOUR LIFE

I always say that building a portfolio is one of the most boring things I do. With **The 3+1 Plan** you **Set and Forget** everything, so there isn't actually that much to do, once you have your portfolio up and running. Purchasing properties is certainly a bit of a thrill, but let's face it, the buying process takes up about 2% of the time you will own it.

It's the holding that you really need to consider and the only reason we hold property is to develop it. Develop the cash flow and develop the capital growth.

THE FOUR WAYS TO CREATE INCOME FROM YOUR PROPERTY

One of the most common questions I get is, *'What's the best way to create income from my property?'* There are four answers:

1. Direct property cash flow

Most people think that best way to create income from an investment property is to have more rent coming in from tenants than is going out through expenses. This is called direct property cash flow, and it has one big downside: income tax. You may get taxed on whatever income you earn in this way. This is one of the reasons we aim for *maximum leverage from our property to help us avoid income tax.* It is important that you work with an accountant to claim the maximum allowable deductions.

2. Selling your property

Another way you can earn large chunks of cash is to sell your property. By doing this, you may be liable for capital gains tax on the increase in value after any allowances. The capital gains tax rulings change often, so you will need to speak to a professional about it. The benefits of selling are that you'll end up with unencumbered cash, once you have taken into account the tax payable and costs.

3. Flipping the property before completion

Flipping involves exchange on an off plan property and prior to completion assigning your interests or subselling to another party. Ideally, this will be for more than you paid for it initially. The profit is yours to keep without having ever owned the property. The disadvantage of this strategy is that unless property prices are increasing, you are at danger of not being able to sell it, or worse still, the property could go down in value.

Normally, flipping creates a capital gain tax liability because you are disposing of an asset.

4. Remortgaging your property

The final and definitely the best way of avoiding or deferring any form of taxation is to refinance or remortgage the property and use the extra capital for whatever purpose you like. As you are using debt to fund this income, you will NOT be subject to income tax or capital gains tax.

Before you jump in and say 'No tax! I'm only ever going to remortgage', in real life you will use all four methods as you build your portfolio. One thing I don't recommend doing is toiling away all your free time on building your portfolio, only to sell it and have to build it again. Remember: you are a ***property investor***, not a ***property manager*** or ***landlord***.

So we know how to earn cash flow from the property, but more important is to know how big your portfolio needs to be in order to run on its own steam.

HOW MANY PROPERTIES BEFORE YOUR PORTFOLIO WILL RUN ON ITS OWN STEAM?

The easy way to answer this question is, 'It varies!' I'll detail the more difficult way below, but it still leads to the same answer as before. There are so many factors at play in your portfolio that no one can say exactly when your portfolio will run on its own steam.

Strategy

This is always the starting point for every portfolio review. The strategy you use will depend on the results you want to achieve. If you are prepared to put the time into researching and finding deals and developing relationships with agents, then you can probably pick up a deal here or there. The specific strategy I use is a 'new build' one. This means that I choose having lots of time over spending all my time, trying to find the best deals that are out there.

What you lose in the deal you pick up is the ease of purchase; what you gain by joining in a bulk deal is the fact that you are putting in very little time, and in most cases, less money into the deal. This frees your time up for lifestyle.

For me, lifestyle is more important than spending a great deal of time constantly pushing for the unrealistic deal.

Structure

How you structure the deal is vital. Using a property investment company means that you can structure the deal in such a way that you can put in as little money as possible, leaving more money to purchase more property. Doing it yourself will generally mean that you will be putting in the full amount, so it will require more time to build momentum.

Stage of cycle

This is fundamental. Assuming the market is in the galloping stage of the cycle, you will normally create significant equity and move to a position of momentum very quickly. If you play your cards right, by the end of this cycle you will be able to operate your portfolio on its own steam. Of course, this always depends on your circumstances and the amount of risk you have managed. Let's face it, over the course of the galloping cycle your property should double in value.

Equity available

Equity is the major determinant as to how fast you can grow your portfolio. If you have £100,000 you will be off and racing a lot quicker than with £25,000 and, of course, if you had £500,000, you will have a massive head start.

Income or cash flow

If you have a £100,000 income versus £18,000 you will obviously be able to move a lot quicker.

There are a few more aspects that we could speak about but in truth, the answer to the original question is simply (and I'm sure very annoyingly), it varies.

I believe that you can set yourself up so that your pension is secured with one cycle of 7–10 years. I truly believe this, and it's why I focus on taking all of my clients from zero to 10 properties.

How long does it take? Well, that's really up to how much you want it.

EXPECTED GROWTH OF YOUR PORTFOLIO

If you consider that property will double every ten years, then it means it must grow 7.2% per year on average. This is assuming that it only doubles every ten years. For it to double every seven years, it would need to be a huge 10.5% compounded annually.

But in truth, it does not grow at 7.2% each and every year. The property cycle we discussed in Chapter 6 affects the rate of growth each year.

Annual % Increase	0	1	2	3	4	5	6	7	8	9	10
5%	£100,000	£105,000	£110,250	£115,763	£121,551	£127,628	£134,010	£140,710	£147,746	£155,133	£162,889
7.50%	£100,000	£107,500	£115,563	£124,230	£133,547	£143,563	£154,330	£165,905	£178,348	£191,724	£206,103
9%	£100,000	£109,000	£118,810	£129,503	£141,158	£153,862	£167,710	£182,804	£199,256	£217,189	£236,736
10.50%	£100,000	£110,500	£122,103	£134,923	£149,090	£164,745	£182,043	£201,157	£222,279	£245,618	£271,408
15%	£100,000	£115,000	£132,250	£152,088	£174,901	£201,136	£231,306	£266,002	£305,902	£351,788	£404,556

You will see from the chart that in order to double ever 7 years you would need an annual % of 10.5% and 10 years would need just under 7.5% per annum

If we factor in the effect of the property cycle over the past fifty years, we find that it has doubled around every 7.3 years. Of those 7.3 years, it will normally decrease or stagnate for one to two years, grow at between 2% to 5% for three to eight years and – best of all – grow between 10% to 25% for between two to three years. Obviously, we all wish every year was a 25% growth year, but there's no way that that could sustain itself.

Armed with this basic knowledge, we can safely and confidently build a portfolio comfortably expecting it will double in the future.

Let's consider a real–life example of two of my clients, David and Mandy. Their property was bought for £135,000 and costs them about £90 per month out of their own pocket. That's £2,160 over two years or approximately £10,000 over ten years.

When Dave and Mandy bought the property, the property cycle was stagnant and therefore they had to fund the property for the first two years. At this stage, they could have remortgaged, as the property was worth £145,000 to £150,000, but they waited another year. They then remortgaged and took out £10,000.

At this point, Dave and Mandy invested just over £3,500 into the property but made a further £6,500. With this £6,500 and some other money that they saved from their income, they bought another property that they let out.

A further two years on and the original property was worth around £160,000. They chose to wait a further two years until they pulled out £12,700. They then bought another property and let it out, so they had three in their portfolio plus their home.

Now it's a further two and a half years down the line, and a funny thing has happened. At their last remortgage, the property that was worth £190,000 has now jumped to £300,000.

At this point, they sold the property for £290,000 and reinvested the capital into a number of other properties. They made £114,000 after all costs and capital gains tax.

Consider the profit from just this one property that they held for nine and a half years. It was £10,000 from the first remortgage, plus £12,700 from the second remortgage, plus £114,000 remaining from the sale proceeds, minus around £11,000 that it cost to hold the property over nine and a half years. This left them £125,000 in profit. Not too bad considering they now have five properties in their portfolio and £125,000 in the bank ready to be invested.

WHAT IS INFLATION? AND HOW DOES IT AFFECT YOUR PORTFOLIO?

One of the things that we haven't covered yet is the effect of inflation on the value of your portfolio. Inflation is one of the things that works for you and against you. Simply defined, inflation is the general rise in prices over time.

A litre of milk that cost £0.15 in 1955 now costs around £1. A loaf of bread costing £0.11 in 1955 now costs £1.25. Average weekly earnings have risen from £31 in 1954 to £580 in 2009.

If prices continue to rise at the same rate over the next thirty-five years, the litre of milk will cost £5.77, the loaf of bread £14.20 and the average weekly wage will be £10,271.60.

We'll all be millionaires but will we be better off? Of course not!

This is why it's important to understand the effects of inflation in terms of your portfolio.

First: inflation will provide you a sure–fire way to refinance your property at regular intervals, allowing you to take out capital regardless of other issues such as supply and demand or market cycles.

Second: inflation will increase the value of the rent you receive, meaning that the value of the cash flow from your property is maintained. This is great news once you retire and are relying on the cash flow from your property portfolio.

Think about a £100,000 house today. If the government instructs the Bank of England to target an inflation rate of 2% to 3% per year and the Bank achieves it on a long term basis, then our house is worth £102,000 in the second year, £105,000 in the third, £107,000 in fourth and £122,000 in the tenth year.

This means we've 'made' £22,000 over ten years. But have we really?

In fact, we have actually not made any money because over the ten years, the amount that £100 of goods bought ten years ago will only buy you the same £100 of goods now, but will cost you £122. So investing based only on inflation isn't a good idea.

But, even though the property only went up by £22,000 over ten years in our example, this is just the inflation proportion of the increase. So if the property doubles in ten years from £100,000 to £200,000, which is what history shows it will do, then the actual real profit will be £200,000 minus £122,000 or £78,000. Still not a bad profit.

Chapter 10

MY SET AND FORGET CHECKLIST
76 CHECKS TO HELP YOU ACHIEVE THE LIFESTYLE YOU WANT

The checklist is where the rubber meets the road for **My Set and Forget Philosophy**. It's in two parts.

The first checklist is the basic stuff that will make building the portfolio very easy; it's the stuff that will ensure that you don't lose money or put yourself or others at risk.

The second part of the checklist will normally be tackled once you have around five properties. It contains all the things that I consider as options to truly **Set and Forget** your portfolio. Most of these things I do religiously in my own portfolio and I recommend that you consider each one very seriously.

My Set and Forget Checklist has come from fourteen years of working with thousands of clients one–on–one and building their portfolios. Originally, the checklist started in my head and, over time, as I added more and more points, I started writing the points into my blog.

Simon Shankland was integral in helping to develop many of the points and I owe a great deal to him. His constant feedback and absolute focus on our clients' needs and emotions has made things so much easier.

I see all of my checklists as organic documents and I'm constantly trying new things, new ways of positively impacting your lifestyle and decreasing the amount of day–to–day work required to manage your portfolio.

The instructions for using the checklist are simple:

Run through each of the points in your own time. How you implement each will depend on the amount of time you want to save and where your emotional intelligence is.

Obviously, my team is trained in the implementation of each of the points and ready to help or refer you to someone in areas that require more specialised knowledge, such as accounting, mortgages and legals.

Some of the points may not have been covered in this book: don't worry, they are all covered in detail on my website, www.3plus1plan.com.

Remember that in this exercise you are taking back valuable time and avoiding many of the problems faced by most investors throughout their journey of achieving **The 3+1 Plan**.

So here we go:

	CATEGORY	SET AND FORGET CHECKLIST – PART A	
1	Accounting	Organising an Accountant	✓
2	Accountant	Knowing what are allowable deductions on your property	✓
3	Bank Accounts	Setting up bank accounts	✓
4	Bank Accounts	All income and rents paid directly into current account	✓
5	Bank Accounts	All expenses and mortgages paid out of current account	✓
6	Bank Accounts	Set up and provide for using a provision account	✓
7	Bank Accounts	Direct debits wherever possible	✓
8	Bank Accounts	Ground rent payments set up	✓
9	Bank Accounts	Service charge payments set up	✓
10	Bank Manager	Upgrade your status at the bank	✓
11	Bank Manager	Meeting your bank manager and getting what you want	✓
12	Cash flow	Mortgage Cost Averaging	✓
13	Debt Reduction	Focussed payment plan for debts	✓
14	EzyTrac	Implementation of EzyTrac Portfolio Management Software	✓
15	EzyTrac	Database of contacts for Portfolio	✓
16	EzyTrac	Tenancy end period updates	✓
17	Filing	Keep all paperwork – Box date system until you file it.	✓
18	Insurance	Insurance policies on loans, mortgages, life insurance	✓
19	Insurance	Household Insurance	✓
20	Insurance	Cash flow an Insurance allowance	✓
21	Landlord	Understanding roles and responsibilities of a landlord	✓
22	Letting your property	How much rent should you be receiving research	✓
23	Letting your property	Managing your letting agents	✓
24	Mortgages	Review mortgage products	✓
25	Mortgages	Basic re-mortgaging principles	✓
26	Psychology	Knowing who to call during 'one of those moments'	✓
27	Psychology	Overstate expenses and understate incomes	✓
28	Review	Setting regular review times	✓
29	Review	Check receipt of rents and income once per month.	✓
30	Review	Check mortgage payments have been paid each month	✓
31	Review	Gas Safety Certificates	✓
32	Lifestyle	Separation of business and personal life	✓
33	Strategy	Cash flow to capital strategy	✓
34	Strategy	Capital to cash flow strategy	✓
35	Support and Review	Specific mentors in place	✓
36	Valuing your Portfolio	How much is your property worth? - Research	✓

Set and Forget Checklist – Part B

So this is the second part of the checklist. I split the checklist into two parts in recognition that having to undertake a full 76 points may be too much for some clients.

	CATEGORY	SET AND FORGET ADVANCED CHECKLIST	
37	Accountant	Exploring tax effective (minimisation) structures	✓
38	Bank Accounts	Upper and lower limits on Current account	✓
39	Bank Accounts	All expenses and mortgages paid in first 10 days of the month	✓
40	Bank Accounts	Setting up coordinated direct debits	✓
41	Bank Accounts	Chequebook used when possible	✓
42	Bank Accounts	Maximum spending with Sleep Test	✓
43	Bank Accounts	Two to sign if discipline needed	✓
44	Bank Accounts	Using ISA account for tax free savings	✓
45	Cash flow	Ensuring accuracy of cash flows	✓
46	Cash flow	Have you allowed for void periods?	✓
47	Credit Cards	How best to use credit cards	✓
48	Credit Cards	Implement charge cards rather than credit cards	✓
49	Credit File	Credit file tracking	✓
50	EzyTrac	Update contact information (managing agents details, letting agents details, etc)	✓
51	Family	Tell your family about what you are doing	✓
52	Family	Looking after mum and dad	✓
53	Family	Investing for the kids	✓
54	Family	An extra family holiday	✓
55	Filing	Sorting out your filing system.	✓
56	Goals	Life planning and goal setting	✓
57	Goals	Personal growth and self improvement	✓
58	International	Building your portfolio internationally	✓
59	Job	Maximising your income at work	✓
60	Market Forces	Understanding interest rates and monetary policy.	✓
61	Market Forces	Understanding the market cycles and impact on cash flow and capital.	✓
62	Mortgages	Practically how do I pull money from my portfolio	✓
63	Mortgages	Explain re-mortgaging when no increase in value of the property strategy.	✓
64	Mortgages	How to calculate the cost of mortgages explanation	✓
65	Mortgages	Principles of mortgage minimisation	✓
66	Mortgages	Restructuring to an offset or all-in-one mortgage account	✓
67	Mortgages	Considering currency and multicurrency mortgages	✓
68	Protection	Exploring protective structures	✓
69	Protection	Considering offshore structures	✓
70	Psychology	Furthering education, breaking down old thought patterns - must read books	✓
71	Psychology	Theoretical knowledge to be applied, how to avoid procrastination.	✓
72	Review	Electrical Safety Certificates	✓
73	Review	Have you raised the rent recently?	✓
74	Simulation	What happens if prices drop by 30% simulation?	✓
75	Simulation	What happens if you were to lose your job simulation?	✓
76	Succession	Organising succession and wills	✓

Chapter 11

THE ONE BIG THING
START YOUR NEW LIFE
WITH ONE GREAT GOAL

It's always fun when I go back to Australia and see the family and friends I grew up with; it's often quite humbling and exciting at the same time.

I had a barbecue for some friends and family to introduce them to my then–fiancé Arlene. Given the situation, my mates took full advantage to tell her about all of my misgivings, embarrassing moments and ex–girlfriends. It then prompted my parents and family to join in.

Well, the dirty laundry was aired and to her credit Arlene still loves me. We are now married. The most interesting bit was looking back at where you came from. One of the stories that I had totally forgotten was when I was a kid and we only had one toothbrush for the family. It wasn't that Mum and Dad were against giving each of us our own toothbrush, it was simply that – like most middle–class families back then – we were cash-strapped.

I wouldn't say we were poor; we were just an average middle-class Australian family in the 1970s. We didn't have a lot, but Mum and Dad worked hard, living from pay check to pay check, and sometimes the pay check didn't extend to the end of the month.

I remember that while still at school, I was working two jobs, the first at McDonalds and then the other at a Foodstore on the weekends. McDonalds paid weekly and the Foodstore was great, because it paid cash at the end of the shift, but regardless of when I got paid, I had spent it by the next pay check.

I have grown up since McDonalds. I now own various companies around the world that pay me a slightly bigger pay check on a monthly basis and regular dividends, as well as money from remortgaging my portfolio. The point is that I still receive a pay check of sorts, but I no longer worry about running out of money or hanging around for my next pay check.

Something changed in my life. I moved from living pay check to pay check to living a life by design. 'By design' I mean 'my design'.

My point is this. It doesn't matter if you had to share your toothbrush as a kid, it doesn't matter if you just got divorced and lost everything. If you're still living from paycheck to paycheck, it means you still have not mastered the fundamentals of money.

Whenever I feel the need, I come back to a book called *The Richest Man in Babylon* by George S. Classon. As the book says:

'If you have not acquired more than a bare existence in the years since we were youths, it is because you either have failed to learn the laws that govern the building of wealth, or else you do not observe them.'

It couldn't be simpler than this. You either don't know the rules or you don't observe them. So which is it? No excuses, no reasons, nothing but the bare naked truth.

If you are living pay check to pay check, then you need to do something different, change something. **The definition of stupidity is doing the same thing over and over and expecting a different result.**

Here's a great way to get some focus on the big picture; 'The One Big Thing' as I like to call it:

The One Big Thing

The one thing I learned through running hundreds of seminars and consulting sessions is this:

The people who get what they want are the people that know what they want.

While I have many ways of expressing what I want, the main focus that I use for my team and me is called **The One Big Thing**.

The **One Big Thing** is more than just a desire; it's a goal. It's a clearly spelled out intention that drives you to think about what life would be like if you focused a bit harder, went the extra mile, pushed yourself a bit further, and were a little less compromising. It's a big goal, a big thing that would change your life.

In 2007, my one big thing was achieving my helicopter pilot license. It was a Big Thing for me. It took sixty hours of actual flying, seven exams from nine different books, a commitment of a half day every week for twelve months, plus study each week. It's something that very few people in the world have done, yet it gives so much freedom.

You may not want to fly helicopters, but I challenge you to pick your One Big Thing this year and achieve it. It may even be buying your first property!

Think back to last year. *What did you really achieve?* Was it just another year in your calendar, or did it see you doing something amazing? Maybe you did. If so, that's fantastic!

But yesterday is the past and, as they say, *'When your past is more exciting than your future, you're a has-been!'*

That may seem a bit harsh, but unfortunately so many people seem to have few goals for the future. People with big, active goals are inspirational. I love spending time with them.

So pick something big, something amazing, something you'll look back on and be proud that you achieved. How do you achieve this One Big Thing? Simply work backwards from the goal and focus on doing the little things.

Personal growth and self improvement

One of the things that I have learned about successful people is that they tend to think like successful people. Over the past five years I have noticed a massive change in the perception of personal development and self–improvement. That stiff upper lip that the English are so famous for is actually starting to loosen a bit.

But personal development doesn't just have to be through reading books, watching the Discovery Channel or attending seminars. In a big way it happens just through living day to day. The challenge I see all too regularly is that rather than living a new day each day, many people live the same routine day in day out, and therefore the amount of personal growth that takes place is limited.

The only way you are going to become a successful property investor is by accepting change and growing on a personal basis.

If you think that just buying property will build you a huge portfolio you are mistaken. The amount of change that you will be faced with will surprise you. The encouraging thing is that you will rarely face anything that you cannot overcome.

The added benefit is that when you have read this book, you'll have all of the technical knowledge you need to achieve **The 3+1 Plan.** The emotional changes you will face will depend on you individually and these lessons are as much a part of the journey as the mistakes we all make along the way.

I love property; it's the one thing that I feel everyone can take equal advantage of. Even though we are all starting at different points, we can all create an amazing lifestyle, a lifestyle of our choosing, a lifestyle by design.

The only real question becomes, 'Will you do it?' Taking action is so important. I have a saying that I use with all of my investors: '*If you don't have a purpose, someone will give you theirs!*'

It is so easy to read this book and come to the end thinking '*What a wonderful book, all the stuff makes sense, I like the ideas and I will get onto that tomorrow.*'

Well that's not good enough: tomorrow you will have other things to worry about. May I suggest that, if you do nothing else, jump onto my website and sign up to my free newsletter. Then write down at least three things you are definitely going to do as a result of reading this book.

Take action, massive action, and you'll be surprised how simple **The 3+1 Plan** is to achieve. Whatever you do, always remember:

Building a portfolio should give you more life.

Live with passion,

BRETT ALEGRE-WOOD

LIST OF WEBSITES TO VISIT

BRETT'S WEBSITES

www.3plus1plan.com

This website contains all of the resources mentioned in the book.

www.YourPropertyClub.com

This is Brett's main educational website and resource for UK investors.

www.YPCWealth.com

This is Brett's FSA–regulated financial planning company specifically aimed at property investors.

www.YPCProperty.com

This is the wholesale sourcing arm of Brett's business, sourcing bulk property all around the UK and supplying to various property investment companies.

www.YPCLettings.com

This is Brett's UK–wide lettings agency, specifically designed to look after the investors interests.

www.EzyTracProperty.com

This is Brett's main site for his free portfolio management software – EzyTrac.

PROPERTY AND DUE DILIGENCE WEB SITES

www.rightmove.com
This is a great website to do all your research and due diligence in the UK.

www.findaproperty.com
Similar to Rightmove.com.

www.houseprices.co.uk
This is a great website that gives you Land Registry data. It may not have the most up-to-date figures, like most of these types of websites they won't have the previous three months figures.

www.nethouseprices.co.uk
Similar to houseprices.co.uk.

www.propertypriceadvice.co.uk
Free online valuation.

www.nhbc.co.uk
The National House Builders Council provides an insurance policy for new homes built under the scheme in the UK.

www.hometrack.co.uk
This website allows you to buy an automated computer valuation for any chosen property in the UK.

www.checkmyarea.com
Search by postcode to find out what type of people live in the area based on demographics such as affluence.

www.checkmyfile.co.uk

Similar to checkmyarea.com, search by postcode for census information, house prices, etc.

www.upmystreet.com

This website provides a heap of information on any postcode in the UK. A great site for your due diligence and research.

www.britishgas.co.uk

Check out the Property Care for Landlords.

maps.google.co.uk

Don't just see it on a map, use the satellite feature to see what the area really looks like.

www.wikipedia.org

Find out what an area is known for, interesting bits of history, famous buildings and so on.

CREDIT REPORTING AGENCIES

www.experian.co.uk

The first of the two main credit reporting agencies that most lenders use.

www.equifax.com

The second main credit reporting agency.

www.callcredit.co.uk

This is a newer and smaller credit agency.

Visit <u>The 3+1 Plan website</u> to find all the resources you need to put the plan into action!

- Free access to *Ezytrac* software

- Download Brett's special reports - learn about the various types of emotional barriers you'll face and how to overcome them

- Find the essential *Set and Forget Checklist* to manage your portfolio

- Read over 200 property articles and the latest property news on Brett's educational blog

- Subscribe to Brett's 'Tips & Tricks' newsletters

www.3plus1plan.com

"Inspired read..."

Belinda and Rakesh - London

Brett's strategy is great for all those cautious investors. There's a focus on getting educated and developing your emotional intelligence and lifestyle. Brett's book is a great introduction to property investment. I have learnt a lot from reading it.

"Property advice to listen to..."

Martin - London

I think the best thing about working with Brett is that he keeps everything very simple but at the same time does not deviate from the principles. He supports and educates you through the emotional and financial aspects of portfolio building. Through this certainty we have been able to secure a portfolio of 9 properties.